The Quickpoint Book

Susan Iglehart and Barbara Schweize

The Quickpoint Book

Holt, Rinehart and Winston   New York

To Philip, Sasha, Laura, and Philip
To Timmy, Nicholas, and Anthony

We would like to thank Elsie Lonsdale, Fran Iglehart, Denny Dale, Freddy Shaw, and Wicky MacColl for their quickpoint work;
Helen Bonsal and Sally Stump for painting canvases;
Lolly Wilson, Dr. B. W. Goat, and Bee Verr for their special help;
Michael Keyser, John Shaw, and John Durand for equipment and expertise;
Billie Conkling, The Blunt Needle, and Hope Hanley for their encouragement.

Photographs and drawings by Susan Iglehart
Lettering by Barbara Schweizer

Published simultaneously in Canada by Holt, Rinehart and Winston of Canada, Limited.

Produced by Chanticleer Press, Inc., New York, N.Y.

Designed by Carol Nehring

Printed in the United States of America.

Contents

PART TWO   PROJECTS

Part One: Basics

The Quickpoint Book gives you all you need to know to take you from start to finish on many different quickpoint projects. We've selected our best designs, ones that we have made ourselves so that we know they work, and we have drawn them to full size so that they are ready to be put on the canvas. We arm you with step-by-step instructions to teach you how to trace our designs right out of the book onto your canvas. Instructions on how to do some interesting stitches especially suited for quickpoint are included. We tell you how to conquer any problem you may run into and how to cope with the expense of completing your pieces by teaching you how to put them together yourself without sacrificing that crisp custom look. In addition, we show you how to create your own personalized designs and your own unique quickpoint projects.

The part of the book called Basics tells you what you need to know about quickpointing: how to prepare your canvas for stitching by tracing and painting the design and how to keep the edge of the canvas from raveling. Also included are numbered steps for doing the quickpoint stitches, some stitches for fun, useful stitches for detail and edge stitches for fastening your project together.

The remainder of the book is made up of quickpoint projects. Each project has a list of the materials you need and the design you will be quickpointing. The project directions give you any specific directions you will need for completing your quickpoint canvas including how to put your dazzling quickpoint item together.

The projects are arranged from very simple to more difficult. Start with an easy project and progress to those more complicated. By the time you have finished all the quickpoint projects you want to make from the book, you will be eager to work out your own ideas for quickpoint projects and we will show you how to do this.

Everything you need to know to make dozens of imaginative items is in this book, as clear and as colorful as quickpoint itself.

What Is Quickpoint?

What is quickpoint? We asked ourselves the same question when we fir heard the word. Quickpoint is big needlepoint worked on large-sca canvas with thick yarn. It is done on the same type of canvas as needlepoi using the same stitches, and it gives you the same results, but in half t time. We are both compulsive needlepointers; however, before we learn about quickpoint, we didn't have enough time to finish all the needlepoi projects we were anxious to do. We wanted to make pillows and racqu covers for our fathers and mothers, handbags for ourselves, dolls and ho by horses for our children, picture frames for Dad and glasses cases f Granny; but we just didn't have time.

Quickpoint to the rescue! In poking through a needlework shop, v came across some needlepoint canvas for rugs (five stitches to the inch) a baskets of thick wool in luscious colors. As soon as we saw this yarn, o fingers were itching to stitch it onto the wonderful king-size canvas. So v plunged right in and worked out designs as we went along. To o delight, the results were sensational. We stitched happily away on o quick needlepoint or quickpoint canvases. Finishing quickpoint gifts time for birthdays was intoxicating. No more half-finished presents. As v experimented, we found that the less expensive rug yarn available variety stores was terrific for quickpoint. It came in clear, bright colo was cooler to work with in the summer than pure wool. It was reasonably priced that we stitched to our hearts' content and we we delighted when our children wanted to make quickpoint pencil cases f school.

We found quickpoint canvases were much more relaxing to work than intricate needlework. No more eyestrain headaches! Quickpoi could be done where smaller needlepoint canvases would have been in possible to work on with any accuracy. It went everywhere: in car poo waiting for planes, watching children at the pool, during football gam and even waiting in the dentist's office. Wherever we went the questi was always the same: What's that? Men, women, and children we fascinated by the chunkiness of the stitches and the brightness of the yar They were astounded by the detail we were able to get on such large-sca needlepoint canvas. Where can we get quickpoint like yours? When v told them we had designed the canvases ourselves, many people wanted to design pieces like the ones we were working on for them. Because their enthusiasm, we were inspired to start painting quickpoint canva and to package them with yarn to sell as kits. At the same time, we ke finding new uses for quickpoint. We went from handbags to pictu frames, from tennis racquet covers to telephone book covers. These ne ideas inspired us to write this book.

Have fun!
Susan Iglehart
Barbara Schweizer

Supplies Needed for Your Projects

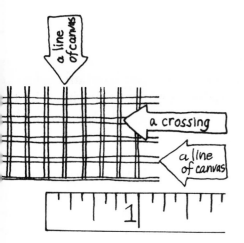

Canvas

Quickpoint canvas, or rug canvas, has five squares to the inch. Ask for No. 5 needlepoint canvas. It is usually available wherever needlework is sold. Each of the projects that follows will tell you exactly how much canvas to buy, allowing for a margin around your design.

Quickpoint canvas is woven with cotton threads which form squares in a regular pattern. The horizontal and vertical threads are arranged in pairs; two threads of canvas form one "line of canvas." The vertical threads are closer together than the horizontal threads. Horizontal lines of canvas crossing vertical lines of canvas form "crossings." Each quickpoint stitch covers a crossing with yarn.

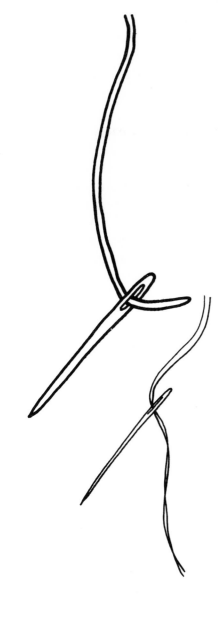

Yarn

Three kinds of yarn can be used for quickpoint: *cotton and rayon rug yarn, rug wool*, and *Persian yarn*. We use the cotton and rayon rug yarn for all our projects because it is inexpensive, durable, and it comes in clear, vibrant colors. Your decision as to which type of yarn to use will depend on the colors available in the stores near you and how much you want to spend. It is best to use one kind of yarn throughout your project.

Cotton and rayon rug yarn is sold in skeins at variety stores and at some needlework stores. It is not expensive; it comes in many bright colors and is long-lasting. You may have to go to more than one store to get all the colors you need. When you use this yarn, buy one skein of each color listed with your project. Each skein consists of several loops. For workable lengths, unfold the skein to form a circle and cut the circle of yarn at one place. Then cut again to make shorter strands. (CAUTION: Some yarns, usually in the red color family, are not completely colorfast. Test all red yarn by threading a needle with yarn and pulling the yarn through a paper towel. Dip the paper towel with yarn attached in cold water. Remove the paper towel and allow it to dry. Has the color run? If so, do not use the yarn.)

Most needlework stores carry wool suitable for quickpoint: *rug wool* and *Persian yarn*. Although wool is more expensive than cotton and rayon rug yarn, it is the finest material for needlework and is also an excellent choice for quickpoint. Persian yarn is sold in strands. Each strand is made up of three threads of yarn twisted together. *Use two strands of Persian yarn for quickpointing*. Since wool suitable for quickpoint is sold in different sized skeins, or by the ounce, it is advisable to take your book or painted canvas with you to the store. Show your design and yarn color list to the salesperson who can tell you how much wool you will need.

Yarn-for-detail: When doing stitches for detail use two threads of Persian yarn, embroidery floss, or any other type of thin yarn.

Needles

At your needlework store, buy a size No. 14 tapestry needle or ask for a needle to use with rug yarn. This size needle is suitable for all types of yarn used for quickpointing. Variety stores carry packages of needles suitable for quickpoint.

When doing the stitches for detail, use a size No. 22 tapestry needle.

Paintbrushes

Any type of small paintbrush can be used for painting on quickpoi[nt] canvas. The best size for tracing the design onto canvas is a No. 1 sal[le] paintbrush and the best size for painting in the colors of the design is a N[o.] 6 sable paintbrush. Sable brushes are expensive but they last forever a[nd] give the best results. Less expensive types of brushes can be used; b[uy] brushes that are equivalent to the sizes of the sable brushes. These a[re] available at art supply stores.

Acrylic Tube Paints

These are available at art supply stores separately or in a set. With a ba[sic] set of acrylic tube paints in primary colors you can mix any color y[ou] need. You may prefer to mix rather than buy a tube of paint in each of t[he] yarn colors. These paints mix with water and are colorfast when dry[.]

Masking Tape

Masking tape is an adhesive paper tape available in various width[s;] purchase a 1-inch wide roll of tape. Tape folded over the edges of yo[ur] canvas will keep the canvas from raveling. Check your project directio[ns] to see if the edges should be taped. Do not tape the edges if your proj[ect] directions tell you to fold under and baste the edges of the canvas.

To tape a canvas, cut a length of tape to equal a side of the canvas. Pla[ce] the tape sticky side up on a flat surface, place the edge of the canvas cove[r]ing one-half inch of the tape. Fold the other half-inch of the tape over t[he] edge of the front of the canvas. Press the tape in place along the entire si[de] of the canvas. Do the same for the remaining three sides of the canva[s.]

Clear Household Cement

Clear household cement is available in tubes at variety stores.

White Household Glue

All-purpose household glue is available in a squeeze bottle at variety stor[es.]

White Paper

To give the bulletin board a clean, white surface for you to work on, cov[er] the bulletin board with any type of white paper. You can use paper towe[ls,] typing paper or a roll of white shelf paper pieced together to cover t[he] bulletin board.

Contact Paper

This is clear plastic with an adhesive back. It is sold in rolls like shelf pap[er] at variety and hardware stores, and you can purchase it in small amount[s.]

Mat Board, Illustration Board

These are both names for a heavy cardboard available at art supply stores [in] various thicknesses. Purchase the 1/8-inch thickness, medium weight f[or] backing the luggage tags.

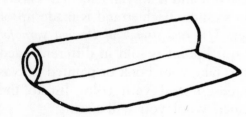

Poster Board (Tag Board) or Blotter Paper

Choose one of these to place between the fabric lining and t[he] quickpointed canvas when making a handbag. White poster board is [a] light cardboard which adds considerable stiffness to a handbag. For a han[d]bag which holds its shape but is more flexible than one made with post[er] board, use a trimmed white desk blotter. These materials are available [at] variety and stationery stores.

Sewing Basket Supplies

Stock your sewing basket with straight pins, safety pins, small sharp scissors, sewing needles, and threads in appropriate colors.

Fabric

We have given generous fabric measurements so you will be sure to have enough. Go ahead and trim the fabric whenever it seems necessary.

Pillow Stuffing

Use polyester fiber fill fluff which is sold in bags at fabric stores.

Bias Tape

A fabric tape available in packages wherever sewing supplies are sold. Purchase wide bias tape which is approximately an inch and a half wide. Bias tape can be used instead of masking tape to keep the edges of the canvas from raveling. When bias tape is folded over the edges of the canvas and machine-stitched in place, it provides a durable and colorful edging for your canvas.

Fold-Over Braid

This is a sturdy decorative edging which is sold folded in half. It is approximately a half inch wide folded and an inch when unfolded. It is available in solid colors by the yard or in packages wherever sewing supplies are sold. Fold-over braid is used in making the tennis racquet cover and in making straps for the carry-all bag.

Fabric Protecting Spray

This spray protects fabric from soil and it is available in spray cans at department stores.

Push Pins, T-shaped Wig Pins

Push pins with long rustproof points are available at stationery or art supply stores. T-shaped wig pins, also called T-pins, are available at fabric stores or beauty supply houses. Push pins or T-shaped wig pins are used to hold the canvas on the bulletin board during painting and during blocking.

Bulletin Board

Purchase a bulletin board made of cork approximately 20 inches by 26 inches at a variety or hardware store. Bulletin boards usually come with a wooden frame; you will only be using the cork surface. The cork surface is used to hold the canvas while you paint the colors of the design on the canvas. The cork surface is also used when you block the completed quickpoint canvas to stretch the canvas back to its original shape.

Basic Techniques

Tracing the Design onto Your Canvas

This is the first step in transferring a design onto the canvas. We do n[ot]
recommend using felt-tip markers or pens for tracing. Even so-called "pe[r]
manent" ones are not always colorfast. Using the fine-tipped No. 1 bru[sh]
and acrylic paint will guarantee colorfastness.

You will need: A roll of clear plastic food wrap
No. 1 sable paintbrush or equivalent
Tube of gray acrylic paint, or a mixture of black and white acrylic pain[t]
Paper cups
Water

Tracing instructions:

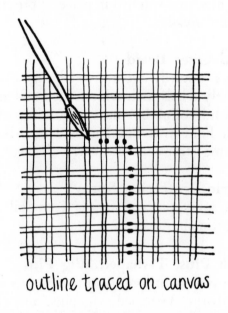

outline traced on canvas

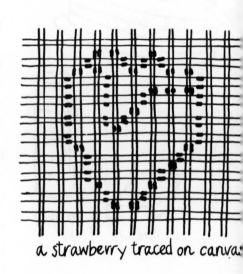

a strawberry traced on canva[s]

1. Cover the design with a piece of clear plastic wrap to protect the boo[k]
2. Mix a dab of paint in a paper cup with a few drops of water. Acryl[ic]
paint mixes with water and is colorfast when dry.
3. Place the canvas over the design in the book, making sure that the ve[r]
tical lines of canvas (threads that are closer together) are running vertical[ly]
in relation to the top of the design. There should be an equal margin [of]
canvas on all sides. Move the canvas slightly, as necessary, so you can s[ee]
clearly all the lines of the design in the book.
4. Dip your brush into the paint and trace the outline of the design on[to]
the canvas with paint.
5. Trace all the lines in the design onto the canvas with paint. Always pai[nt]
the threads of canvas which are over the lines of the design in the boo[k.]
The illustration above right shows what your canvas will look like wi[th]
lines traced on it. (You will paint in the colors of the design later.) As y[ou]
trace, check from time to time to be sure the canvas has not shifted.
6. If you are doing a design that covers more than one page, paint the ou[t]
line and all the lines within the design on the first page before going to t[he]
next page. Re-position the canvas on the second page of the design so th[at]
the painted outline on the canvas will connect with the outline of the s[ec]
ond page. Paint the outline from the second page, then the lines in t[he]
design. Follow the same procedure if the complete design runs to thr[ee]
pages.

Painting in the Colors of Your Design

After you have traced the lines of the design onto the canvas, paint in the areas of color so that you will know where to stitch the different colors of yarn. The design in the book indicates what color to paint. Use the color photograph of the project as a guide in choosing shades of color.

You will need:

Bulletin board
White paper to cover the cork surface of the board
Push pins
Acrylic paint to match each color of yarn
Water
Paper cups for mixing paints
No. 6 sable paintbrush or equivalent

Painting instructions:

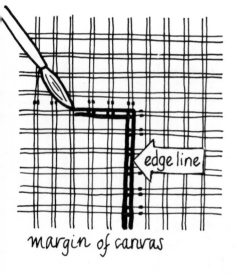

edge line

margin of canvas

1. Place white paper over the cork surface of the bulletin board (within the frame if your bulletin board has one) and anchor the paper in place with a push pin in each corner. Place the canvas on the bulletin board and anchor the canvas flat against the paper with push pins.
2. Mix paint in each of the yarn colors by squeezing a fingertip of paint into a paper cup and mixing thoroughly with a few drops of water. Rinse your brush in water before you change colors in order to keep the paint clear and bright.
3. Paint the smallest shapes of the design first—airplane, flowers, small trees, etc. Some small shapes are only one stitch big so you should paint the corresponding color on only one crossing of the canvas. You will find you are painting the crossings within the lines you traced onto the canvas as if you were coloring a child's coloring book.
4. The first line of canvas within the traced outline of the design is the *edge line.* Paint the remaining areas of color of the design until you have covered the canvas including the edge line. However, if your project's directions specify what color to paint the edge line, first paint the edge line accordingly, then finish painting the colors of the design.
5. Let the painted canvas dry completely.

Hints to improve your painting skills:

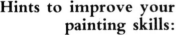

painting a crossing

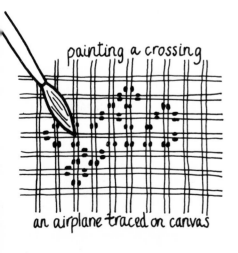

an airplane traced on canvas

A well-painted canvas has no white canvas showing through the paint.
★ Keep in mind in choosing or mixing colors that the color will be slightly darker when the paint dries than when it is wet.
★ A plastic squeeze bottle filled with water is a convenient container to use when mixing paint, since it allows you to add a drop or two at a time.
★ Experience will make you a master at mixing paint to the right consistency. You may find it is easier to paint two light coats to achieve the results you desire.
★ If you find that the paint is not covering the canvas smoothly, add a drop or two of water to the paint. Do not dilute the paint too much, however, or it will soak through to the wrong side of the canvas. If the paint does soak through in any area, wait until it dries, then lightly touch up the back of the canvas with white paint.
★ Be careful to paint the crossings of the canvas so you will know exactly where to stitch.
★ You can keep mixed paints from drying up for a short time by covering paper-cup containers with plastic wrap. To keep paints moist for a few days, store them in small glass jars with lids.
★ After each use, wash your brushes with soap and water, then reshape the bristles. Store your brushes in an open jar with bristle ends up.

13 Basic Techniques

Folding Under and Basting the Margin of Canvas

The canvas of certain projects needs the special preparation of folding under and basting the margin of canvas around the design. This step must be done before quickpointing the design. Your project directions will tell you if you should fold under and baste the margin of canvas.

Instructions:

1. Trim the canvas so that there is a 1½-inch margin of unpainted canvas around the design. Trim the tips of the corners diagonally.

2. Fold under the margin of canvas so that the edge line (page 13, step 4) the outer perimeter of your painted design. As you fold each side, be careful to follow the same line of canvas.

3. With quickpoint yarn and needle, baste the two layers of canvas together 1/2-inch in from the edge line. As you baste, pull the yarn so that the squares of the painted canvas line up with those of the margin of canvas underneath, and the two layers of canvas are flat against each other. There is now a margin of unpainted canvas showing around your painted design. quickpointing, you will stitch through the two layers as if they were one. Pull out the basting as you quickpoint.

4. Do not quickpoint *over* the edge line. Your project directions will tell you when to stitch the edge line. You will either decorate the edge line with an edge stitch or join two edge lines with an edge stitch.

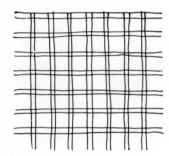

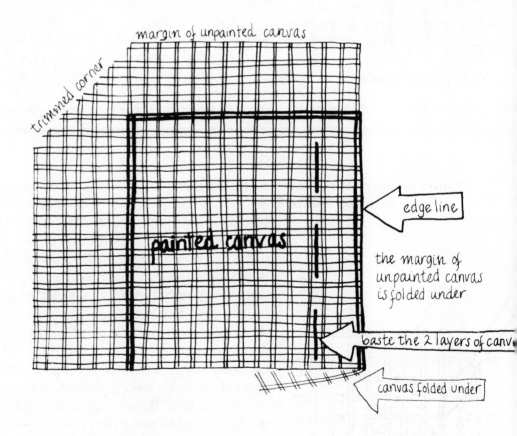

margin of unpainted canvas

trimmed corner

edge line

painted canvas

the margin of unpainted canvas is folded under

baste the 2 layers of canvas

canvas folded under

Blocking

Blocking puts your complete canvas back into its original shape and smooths both the yarn and the canvas.

You will need: Bulletin board
White paper
Pencil
Ruler
Terry-cloth bath towels
T-shaped wig pins or rustproof push pins
Fabric protecting spray

Instructions: 1. Cover the cork surface of the bulletin board up to the frame with white paper. Measure the worked quickpoint. With a pencil draw an outline 1/2-inch bigger than the worked quickpoint on the white paper.
2. Dip your quickpointed canvas into a sink full of cold water. Take the canvas out immediately and roll in a terry-cloth towel to remove excess moisture. Blot the canvas four more times using dry towels.
3. Lay the damp quickpoint canvas on the bulletin board within the pencil lines and gently pull the canvas back to its original shape.
4. Measure the parallel sides to be sure they are equal. Using the pencil lines around the worked quickpoint as a guide, push the pins through the edge lines of the canvas making sure the rows of stitches are straight; the stretched worked quickpoint will not reach the pencil lines. Pin every quarter of an inch to insure that the sides will dry straight. If you are working with a taped canvas, pin through the margin of unworked canvas keeping the rows of quickpoint straight and the shape of the project symmetrical.
5. Leave the canvas on the board until it is absolutely dry. It may take a day or two for your canvas to dry completely. An electric fan will help to speed up drying.
6. Spray the dry quickpoint with fabric protecting spray to keep it looking bright.

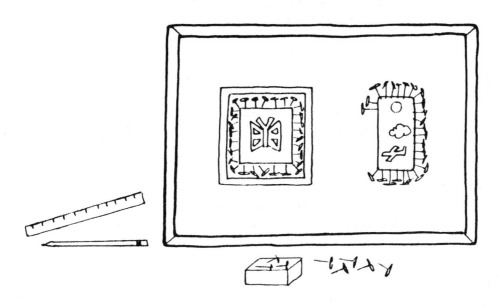

Quickpoint Stitches

The quickpoint stitch is a large needlepoint stitch on king-size canvas wi[th] thick yarn. There are two ways to do the quickpoint stitch: the Contine[n]tal and the Basketweave. Both cover your canvas with rows of slanti[ng] stitches, all of which slant in the same direction. The Continental is t[he] easiest stitch for a beginner. It is always worked horizontally across t[he] canvas from right to left. The Basketweave is a sturdier stitch than t[he] Continental. It is a little more difficult, but once you have learned how [to] do it, you will find it is more interesting than the Continental. T[he] Basketweave stitch is worked *diagonally* and is the best stitch to use f[or] quickpoint. To insure that all of your stitches will slant in the right dire[c]tion, mark the top of your canvas with a safety pin or tie on a bit of ya[rn] before you start to stitch.

★ The illustrations show the stitches smaller than your stitches will be [so] that you can see the exact location of each stitch. Although the illustratio[ns] show lines of canvas between each stitch, you will not see lines of canv[as] between your completed quickpoint stitches.

The Continental Stitch

First row:

1. With the top of the canvas up, bring the threaded needle up throug[h] square of the canvas. This is Square 1. Now push the needle down throu[gh] the canvas at Square 2 which is one square to the right of and above t[he] square the needle came through. A slanting stitch will cover a crossing [of] the canvas.

2. Bring the needle up through the canvas at Square 3 which is one squa[re] to the left of Square 1. Stitch over the crossing, pushing the needle dov[n] through Square 4, which is one square to the left of Square 2.

3. Bring the needle up through the canvas at Square 5, which is one squa[re] to the left of Square 3. Stitch over the crossing, pushing the needle dov[n] through Square 6, which is one square to the left of Square 4.

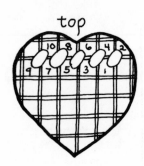

4. Bring the needle up through the canvas at Square 7, which is one squa[re] to the left of Square 5. Stitch over the crossing, pushing the needle dov[n] through Square 8, which is one square to the left of Square 6.

5. Bring the needle up through the canvas at Square 9, which is one squa[re] to the left of Square 7. Stitch over the crossing, pushing the needle dov[n] through Square 10, which is one square to the left of Square 8. You ha[ve] now completed five quickpoint stitches.

6. Come up again at Square 7, which is one square below Square 10. *Tu[rn] the canvas around.*

Second row:

In quickpoint, each square of canvas holds yarn from two different stitch[es]. Square 7 now has yarn from a stitch in your first row and yarn from wh[at] will be your first stitch in the second row.

1. Push the needle down at Square 11, which is one square up and o[ne] square to the right of Square 7 and directly above Square 9.

2. Come up at Square 5 and stitch over the crossing, pushing the nee[dle] down at Square 12, which is one square to the left of Square 11.

3. Come up at Square 3 and stitch over the crossing, pushing the nee[dle] down at Square 13, which is one square to the left of Square 12.

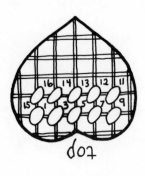

4. Come up at Square 1 and stitch over the crossing, pushing the nee[dle] down at Square 14, which is one square to the left of Square 13.

5. Come up at Square 15, which is directly above Square 2, stitch over the crossing and go down at Square 16, which is one square to the left of Square 14. You have now completed your second row of quickpoint stitches.

6. Come up at Square 17, which is one square above Square 16. *Turn the canvas around* at the end of each row and continue to stitch until the design is completely covered with quickpoint stitches.

The Basketweave Stitch

First row:

1. Bring the needle through a square in the canvas. This is Square 1. Push the needle down through the canvas at Square 2, which is one square above and one square to the right of the square the needle came up through. A slanting stitch will now be covering a crossing.

2. Bring the needle up through Square 3, which is two squares below Square 2. Stitch over the crossing, pushing the needle down through Square 4, which is one square above and one square to the right of Square 3.

3. Bring the needle up through the canvas at Square 5, which is two squares below Square 4. Stitch over the crossing, pushing the needle down through Square 6, which is one square above and one square to the right of Square 5.

4. Bring the needle up through the canvas at Square 7, which is two squares below Square 6. Stitch over the crossing, pushing the needle down through Square 8, which is one square above and one square to the right of Square 7.

5. At this point, you can see that the yarn is covering the crossings and that all of the stitches align in one diagonal row of four quickpoint stitches. To do your next diagonal row, you will work *back up* towards Square 1.

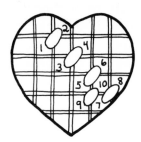

Second row:

1. Bring the needle up at Square 9, which is one square to the left of Square 7. Stitch over the crossing, pushing the needle down through Square 10, which is one square above and one square to the right of Square 9. You will be forming two interlocking rows of stitches.

2. Bring the needle up through Square 11, which is two squares to the left of Square 10. Stitch over the crossing, pushing the needle down through Square 12, which is one square above and one square to the right of Square 11.

3. Bring the needle up through Square 13, which is two squares to the left of Square 12. Stitch over the crossing, pushing the needle down through Square 14, which is one square above and one square to the right of Square 13.

4. Bring the needle up through Square 15, which is two squares to the left of Square 14. Stitch over the crossing, pushing the needle down through Square 16, which is one square above and one square to the right of Square 15. You have now completed your second diagonal row of stitches.

5. Bring the needle up at Square 17, which is one square below Square 15 and continue to stitch.

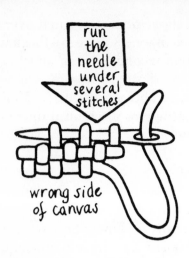

run the needle under several stitches

wrong side of canvas

Starting and Ending Strands of Yarn

Use strands of yarn that are about 20 inches long and experiment to se what length of yarn you like best.

★ Knots are never used in quickpoint.

To *start a strand of yarn*, bring the needle up through the square you wis to use as your starting point leaving an inch tail on the wrong side of th canvas. Do not pull the tail through. Begin to quickpoint, catching the ta within the stitches as you work.

To *end a strand* of yarn, push the needle through to the wrong side of th canvas and run the needle under several adjacent stitches. Pull the need through and cut off the remaining yarn.

Quickpointing Hints

As you quickpoint, check to see how your stitches are covering the canva The yarn should completely cover the canvas. If you see canvas showir through, it may be due to one or more of the following:

★ You may be pulling the yarn too tightly as you stitch. If you are usir long strands of yarn, the yarn can become thin from being pulled throug the canvas many times. Try using shorter strands.

★ Quickpointing tends to twist the strands of yarn, making it appear thi Let go of your needle from time to time and allow the yarn to untwis

Stitches for Fun

These stitches add variety to your quickpointing. They are a decorativ way to add texture to large areas of solid color and an interesting chang from the Basketweave or Continental stitch. Some of these stitches cov more than one line of canvas so your work will go quickly. The proje directions suggest where these stitches can be used, but you can use the anywhere you want to.

Interlocking Gobelin Stitch

This stitch can be used for the Hobbyhorse, and evergreen trees and hills the Design-It-Yourself pillows.

Bring your needle up through the canvas at Square 1 and go dov through the canvas at Square 2. Your stitch covers two crossings. Bring th needle up at Square 3, which is one square to the right of Square 1, and down through the canvas at Square 4 which is one square to the right Square 2. Bring the needle up at Square 5 which is one square to the rig of Square 3 and go down through the canvas at Square 6 which is o square to the right of Square 4. Continue to work in this way coverir two crossings with each stitch until you have finished the row, then end the yarn.

Start the second row by bringing the needle up at the square which one square below Square 1 and go down through the canvas at the squa which is one square below Square 2. Continue to stitch until you ha completed the second row, then end off the yarn. Continue to stit starting at the third row. Follow the sequence of stitches as you wor

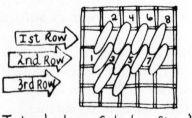

Interlocking Gobelin Stitch

1st Row 2nd Row 3rd Row

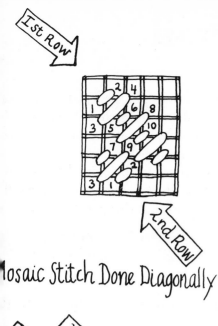

Mosaic Stitch Done Diagonally

Mosaic Stitch Done Diagonally

This stitch can add texture to the mane of the Lion Glasses Case and the hills and mountain sides of the Design-It-Yourself pillows.

To start the first row, bring your needle up through the canvas at Square 1 and go down through the canvas at Square 2. Come up through Square 3, which is one square below Square 1, and go down again through Square 4, which is one square to the right of Square 2. Next, bring the needle up through Square 5, which is one square to the right of Square 3, and go down through Square 6, which is one square below Square 4. Continue to stitch, alternating between covering one crossing, and two crossings, until you have finished the row; then end off the yarn. Start the second row with a stitch covering one crossing where it will line up diagonally with a stitch covering two crossings (see illustration).

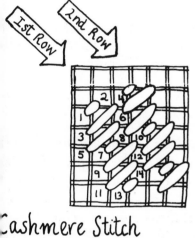

Cashmere Stitch

Cashmere Stitch

This stitch is suitable only for large areas of solid color such as the hills and mountain sides of the Design-It-Yourself pillows.

Bring your needle up through the canvas at Square 1 and go down through the canvas at Square 2. Continue to stitch until you have finished the row, then end off the yarn. Start the second row by bringing the needle up at Square 4. Continue to stitch until you have completed the second row, then end off the yarn. Continue to stitch always starting at the top and working down in diagonal rows.

oing the Surrey Stitch

Surrey Stitch

The Surrey stitch is used on the tip of the tail on the Lion Glasses Case. It can also be used to add texture to the centers of flowers and to make tufts of grass.

Push the needle down at Square 1 and bring the needle up at Square 2 leaving an inch tail of yarn on the right side of the canvas. Circle the yarn around the tail as shown in the illustration. Push the needle down at Square 3 and come up through the canvas at Square 1, making sure the needle goes over the circle of yarn. Pull the needle and yarn through tightly. Cut off the yarn at half an inch for the lion's tail and as short as you want for other uses.

the completed Surrey Stitch

Stitches for Detail

The dotted lines on the designs show you where to place the stitches for detail. Do these embroidery stitches on your completed and blocked quickpoint canvas to add finishing touches such as kite strings and blades o grass. Use a No. 22 tapestry needle and yarn-for-detail which is two strands of Persian yarn or any other type of thin yarn. Use quickpoint yar and needle for thicker stitches, such as hair on the Design-It-Yourself figures. The project directions tell you what color and type of yarn to us and which Stitch for Detail to do.

Straight Stitch

This stitch is used to make blades of grass and hair for the figures on the Design-It-Yourself pillows.

Bring the needle up through the canvas where you want one end of th stitch to be, then push the needle down where you want the other end the stitch to be. This stitch can be made in varied lengths.

Straight Stitch

Back Stitch

This stitch is used to make thin lines for details such as the kite string on th Design-It-Yourself pillow and the rays of the sun on the Airplane Lugga Tag, the mouth and claws on the Lion Glasses Case, and the initials on th Envelope Handbag.

Bring the needle up a quarter of an inch from where you want the stitc to start, point 1. Go back and push the needle down at 2. Bring the need up at 3 and go back down at 1 again. Continue to stitch in this way to for a straight or curved line.

Back Stitch

French Knot

This stitch is used on the Strawberry Pincushion, the Flower Doorsto and on the Bunny Picture Frame to make the bunnies' tails.

Bring the needle up where you want the French knot to be. Hold t needle close to the quickpointed canvas and wind the yarn around the ne dle three or four times. Push the needle down through the canvas close where the yarn came up.

French Knot

Edge Stitches

The whipstitch or the binding stitch are used to finish or put together quickpoint projects. These stitches can only be used if the edges of the canvas have been folded under and basted as described on page 14. You can use either of these stitches to join two edge lines of quickpoint or to decorate a single edge line. The whipstitch is easy to master; the binding stitch is a bit more difficult but makes a handsome braided edge. Use the color yarn indicated in each project or choose a color that will blend or accent your finished piece.

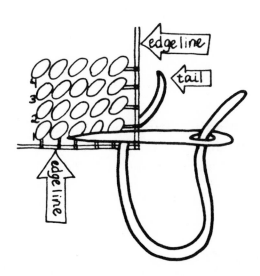

The Whipstitch

The Whipstitch on One Edge Line

Anchoring the first strand of yarn for the whipstitch:

1. Holding the edge line of your worked quickpoint, bring the needle through Square 1 of the edge line, leaving an inch tail of yarn.
2. Carry the yarn over the edge line. Push the needle through Square 1 again.

Doing the whipstitch on one edge line:

1. Carry the yarn over the edge line and push the needle through Square 2, catching the tail of yarn within the stitch to secure it.
2. Carry the yarn over the edge line and push the needle through Square 3.
3. Carry the yarn over the edge line and push the needle through Square 4.
4. Continue to do the whipstitch, always pushing your needle from right to left.

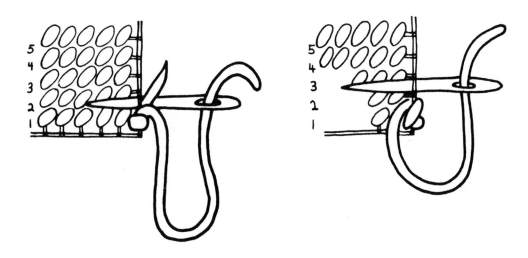

The Whipstitch Joining Two Edge Lines

Anchoring the first strand of yarn for the whipstitch:

1. Hold the two edge lines together and line up Square 1 of the right-ha[nd] edge line with Square 1 of the left-hand edge line. Push the needle throu[gh] Square 1 of the *left-hand* edge line, leaving an inch tail of yarn.
2. Carry the yarn over both edge lines; push the needle through Squar[e 1] of the right-hand edge line, then through Square 1 of the left-hand e[dge] line. (This will be the second time you have come through Square 1 of [the] left-hand edge line.)

Doing the whipstitch on two edge lines:

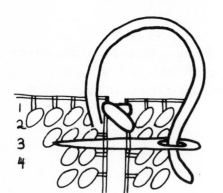

1. Carry the yarn over both edge lines; push the needle through Squar[e 2] of the right-hand edge line, then through Square 2 of the left-hand e[dge] line.
2. Carry the yarn over both edge lines; push the needle through Squar[e 3] of the right-hand edge line, then through Square 3 of the left-hand e[dge] line.
3. Continue to whipstitch, matching each square of the right-hand ed[ge] line with the corresponding square of the left-hand edge line, movi[ng] down one square with each stitch. The yarn tail will be secured betwe[en] the edges as you stitch.

The Binding Stitch on One or Two Edge Lines

The binding stitch, while most often used to fasten pieces of a quickpo[int] project together, can also be used to decorate one edge line. Simply wo[rk] the sequence of stitches on a single edge line. When doing the bindi[ng] stitch, the needle always goes from right to left.

Anchoring the first strand of yarn for the binding stitch:

1. Holding the two edges of worked quickpoint together, bring the need[le] through Square 1 of the left-hand edge line, leaving an inch tail of yar[n.]
2. Matching squares exactly, push the needle through Square 1 of the rig[ht-] hand edge line and through Square 1 of the left-hand edge line. (This is t[he] second time you have come through the left-hand Square 1.)
3. Go through the right-hand Square 2, below Square 1, and through t[he] matching Square 2 of the left-hand edge line catching the tail of ya[rn] within the stitch to secure it.
4. Go back up and push the needle through Square 1 of the right-ha[nd] edge line again and through Square 1 of the left-hand edge line aga[in.]

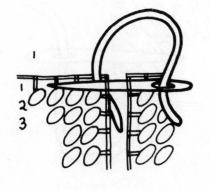
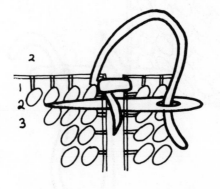
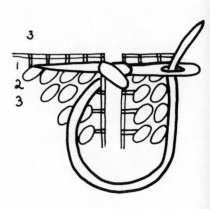

Doing the binding stitch: **1.** Go down two squares and push the needle through the right-hand Square 3, then through the matching Square 3 of the left-hand edge line.
2. Go up one square and push the needle through the right-hand Square 2, then through the matching square 2 of the left-hand edge line.
3. Go down two squares and push the needle through the right-hand Square 4, then through the matching Square 4 of the left-hand edge line.
4. Go up one square and push the needle through the right-hand Square 3, then through the matching Square 3 of the left-hand edge line.
5. Go down two squares and push needle through the right-hand Square 5, then through matching Square 5 of the left-hand edge line.
6. Go up one square and push the needle through the right-hand Square 4, then through the matching Square 4 of the left-hand edge line.

Keep repeating the preceding pattern of stitches: "down two squares and up one square." You will begin to see the braided pattern shown in the accompanying illustration. When starting a new strand of yarn, bring the needle up continuing the pattern of stitches catching the tail as you stitch. Continue the binding stitch until the pieces of your project are fastened together.

The binding stitch can also be done from bottom to top in the same manner, but the pattern of stitches will be: "up two squares and down one square."

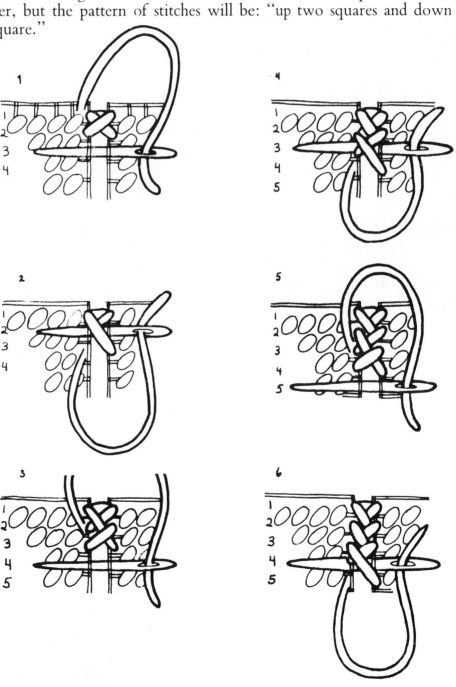

Sewing Stitches

You will sometimes use sewing stitches in finishing your projects. T
project's directions will tell you which stitch to use.

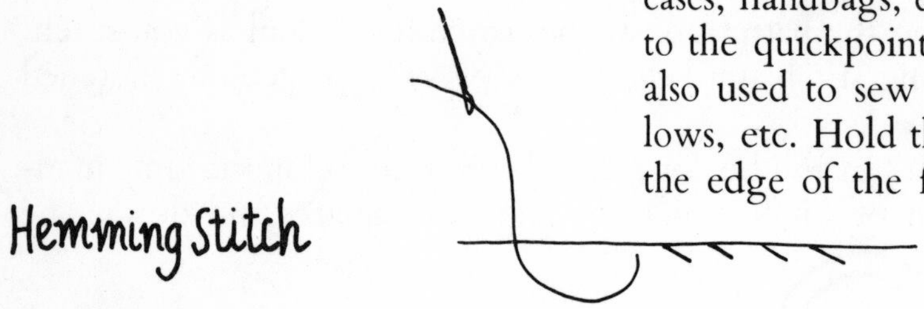

Hemming Stitch
The hemming stitch is used to sew fabric lining in glasses cases, per
cases, handbags, etc. With sewing needle and thread, sew the fabric lin
to the quickpoint as if you were hemming a skirt. The hemming stitc
also used to sew two edges together in projects such as pincushions, j
lows, etc. Hold the two edges together and do the hemming stitch to s
the edge of the fabric to the edge of the quickpoint.

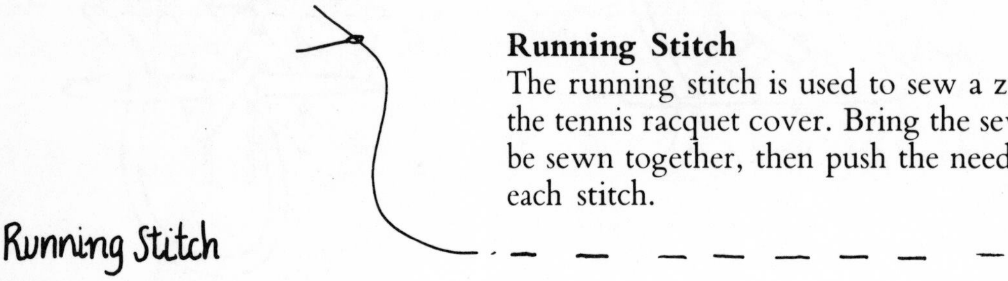

Hemming Stitch

Running Stitch
The running stitch is used to sew a zipper in the pencil case and to ma
the tennis racquet cover. Bring the sewing needle up through the pieces
be sewn together, then push the needle down through the pieces to ma
each stitch.

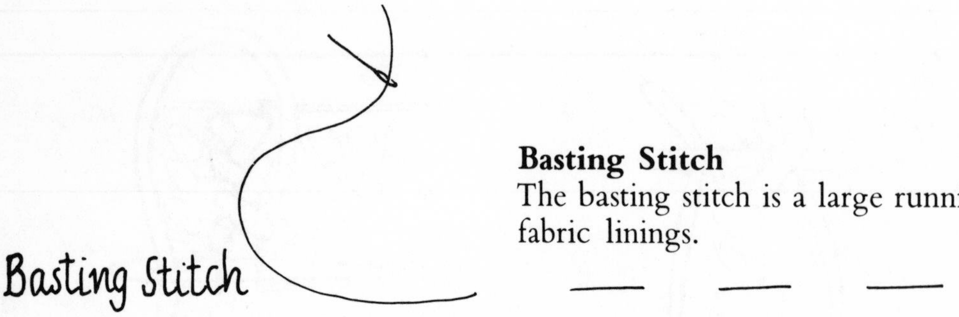

Running Stitch

Basting Stitch
The basting stitch is a large running stitch used in all projects which ha
fabric linings.

Basting Stitch

Right. Work in progress: Geranium Design painted on canvas with
margin of canvas folded under and partially basted; Strawberry Desi
traced on canvas and partially painted; House Handbag and strap partia
put together with the binding stitch; Airplane Luggage Tag with fol
edge; and Butterfly Pincushion with taped edge being blocked with
pins.

Above.
Flower Brick Bookend; Butterfly Pincushion; Strawberry Pincushio
Butterfly Pincushion Design in a Quickpoint Kit; Manilla Luggage Ta

Right Above.
Envelope Handbag with ribbon strap; Tulip Picture Frame; back
manilla-colored Envelope Handbag; Bunny Picture Frame

Right.
Matisse Handbag, Ribbons, a Versatile Design, as a handbag; Wov
Basket, a Versatile Design, as a tennis racquet cover

Above.
Hobbyhorse

Right Above.
Patchwork, a Versatile Design, as a large envelope handbag; Lion Glasse
Case; Dirndl Doll; Green Valley Pencil Case; Rainbow Handbag; Hous
Handbag

Right.
Patchwork, a Versatile Design, as a large envelope handbag being blocke
with T-pins

Above.
Tennis Racquet Cover; Airplane Luggage Tag; Indian, a Versatile Desig
as a handbag

Right.
Lion Glasses Case; Geranium Telephone Book Cover; Navajo Carry-A
Bag

Overleaf.
Design-It-Yourself Pillows: Seaside Design, Hillside Design, Mountainsi
Design made into a carry-all bag

Part Two: Projects

Each project tells you everything you need to know to make pincushions, pencil cases, picture frames, and more. Even if you have never held a paintbrush before, you can trace the designs onto your canvas right out of the book and then paint in the colors as if you are coloring in a child's coloring book. Once you start to stitch the wonderful king-size canvas with colorful quickpoint yarn, you will be a quickpointer forever! The project directions tell you how to make the completed quickpoint canvas into a finished item *yourself.* Remember to turn to Part One if you need more detailed information.

Pincushions

In an hour you can stitch a delightful pincushion to decorate your dress, add to your sewing basket, or give to a friend.

You will need: No. 5 quickpoint canvas, 7 inches by 7 inches
No. 14 tapestry needle for rug yarn
Strawberry design: yarn in red, pale blue, green;
yellow yarn-for-detail with No. 22 tapestry needle
Butterfly design: yarn in red, pink, yellow, green
Fabric for the back, 8 inches by 8 inches
Forty cotton balls
Sewing needle and thread
3/4-yard eyelet lace to trim pincushion (optional)

Directions: 1. Trace and paint the design onto the canvas as described on pages 12-1
2. Fold masking tape over the edges of the canvas (page 10).
3. Quickpoint the design.
4. Block the quickpointed canvas.
5. Stitches for detail: on the *Strawberry* pincushion, embroider French kno
on the strawberries with yellow yarn-for-detail.
6. Cut the fabric for the back of the pincushion so that it is the same size
the canvas. If you want to trim a pincushion with eyelet lace: with rig
side of the quickpointed canvas up, baste the lace to the quickpoint stitc
nearest the margin of canvas as shown in the illustration.
7. Place right sides of the fabric and quickpointed canvas togeth
Machine sew around three sides of the pincushion, turning the corners
the fourth side but leaving an opening for stuffing on the fourth side of t
pincushion.
8. Trim the canvas and fabric to within one inch of the worked quickpo
and trim the corners diagonally. Turn the pincushion right side out.
9. Stuff the pincushion with cotton balls. With sewing needle and threa
use the hemming stitch to close the pincushion.

Strawberry design

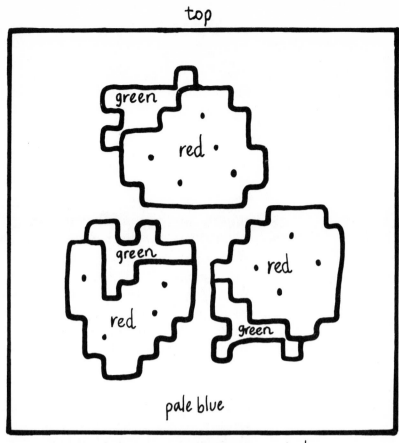

top

green

red

green

red

red

green

pale blue

··· dots show Stitches for Detail ···

Butterfly design

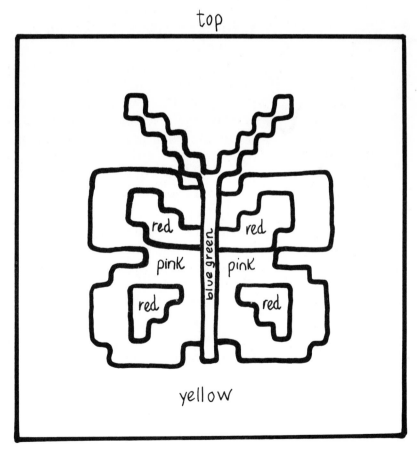

top

red   red

blue green

pink   pink

red   red

yellow

Luggage Tags

Since airline regulations now require identification tags on all suitcases, luggage tag is an ideal gift for your friends who travel.

You will need: No. 5 quickpoint canvas 6 inches wide by 8 inches long for each tag
No. 14 tapestry needle for rug yarn
Manilla luggage tag design: yarn in dark orange and beige
Airplane luggage tag design: yarn in yellow, light blue, white, gray;
yellow yarn-for-detail with No. 22 tapestry needle
Mat board, 3 inches by 5 inches
Clear household cement
Waterproof marker or ballpoint pen
Clear plastic contact paper or 1½-inch wide clear transparent tape
Sharp-pointed instrument, such as ice pick
String, 1/8-inch thick and 14 inches long

Directions: 1. Trace and paint the design onto the canvas as described on pages 12-1
On the *Manilla* luggage tag canvas paint the center of the dark orange ci
cle beige. On the *Airplane* luggage tag canvas paint the edge line yellov
2. Fold under and baste the margin of canvas (page 14).
3. Quickpoint the design. On the *Manilla* luggage tag work the dar
orange circle first. On the *Airplane* luggage tag work the sun, cloud, ar
airplane then fill in the background.
4. Block the quickpointed canvas.
5. Stitches for detail: on the *Airplane* luggage tag embroider the rays of tl
sun with yellow yarn-for-detail using the back stitch.
6. Whipstitch around the edge line of the canvas with beige yarn for tl
Manilla luggage tag or with yellow yarn for the *Airplane* luggage ta;
starting at the lower right-hand corner.

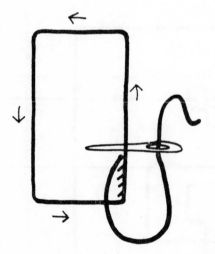

7. Trim the mat board to measure the exact size of your quickpoint ta;
Write the name and address on the mat board with a waterproof marker c
ballpoint pen. Cover the writing with a piece of clear plastic conta
paper, folding it smoothly around the edges to the back of the mat boar
8. Spread clear household cement on the back of the quickpoint and plac
the quickpoint on top of the back of the mat board. To insure that tl
quickpoint will dry smoothly, place books on top of the tag for sever
hours until the cement dries.
9. Make a hole with the ice pick in the center of the orange circle on tl
Manilla luggage tag and in the center of the sun on the *Airplane* luggag
tag. For the *Airplane* luggage tag, you can paint the string with yello
acrylic tube paint before you thread it through your tag. Thread a tapestr
needle with the string and push the needle through the hole to create a t
for the luggage tag. Now your tag is ready to go!

Manilla luggage tag design

top

dark

orange

beige

Airplane design

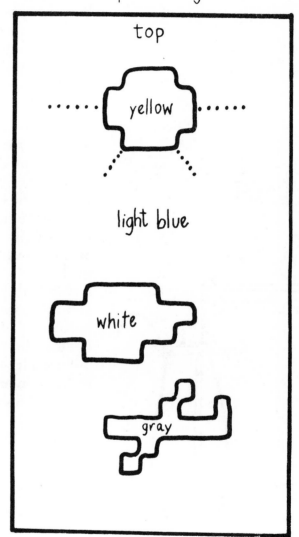

top

yellow

light blue

white

gray

··· dots show Stitches for Detail ··

Lion Glasses Case

The Lion glasses case gives you an opportunity to use some of the Stitch[es] for Fun. The Mosaic stitch gives the lion's mane texture and the lion's bac[k] is as cute as his front with Surrey stitch worked on the tip of his tail. Li[ne] your glasses case with a bright fabric to delight you every time you p[ut] your glasses into the lion.

You will need: Two pieces of No. 5 quickpoint canvas, each 7 inches wide by 9½ inch[es] long
No. 14 tapestry needle for rug yarn
Yarn in light orange, dark orange, yellow, brown, off-white
Brown yarn-for-detail with No. 22 tapestry needle
Fabric for lining, 8 inches by 8 inches
Sewing needle and thread

Directions: 1. Trace and paint the design onto the canvases as described on pages 12–1[3]
When tracing the design, do the lion's eyes first. Each eye is two crossin[gs] wide. Paint the edge line orange.

2. Fold under and baste the margin of each of the canvases separately (pa[ge] 14). Do not sew the two pieces of your glasses case together at this tim[e.]

3. Quickpoint the design starting with the lion's face. Work the mane ne[xt] in Mosaic stitch. On the lion's back, stitch the mane first, then the ta[il.] Work the tip of the tail in Surrey stitch. Complete the lion in Quickpoi[nt] stitch.

4. Block the quickpointed canvases.

5. Stitches for detail: embroider the claws and mouth in back stitch usin[g] brown yarn-for-detail.

6. Hold the front and back of the glasses case together with *right sides o[ut.]* Whipstitch the two edge lines together with dark orange yarn (or chan[ge] to light orange as you work to match the design.) Be sure to match t[he] squares of the two edge lines as you stitch. Start at the top of the right-ha[nd] side and whip down the side, across the bottom, up the other side, the[n] around the top edges of the glasses case opening. Be careful not to stitc[h] your glasses case closed.

7. Fold the lining fabric in half and trim the width to the same size as t[he] width of the glasses case.

8. With sewing needle and thread, baste the sides and bottom 1/2 in[ch] from the edge of the fabric. Try the lining in the glasses case for fit. T[he] lining should fit smoothly with no wrinkles or folds. Remove the bast[ed] lining from the glasses case.

9. If the lining was too large for a smooth fit, machine sew within the li[ne] of basting, so that the finished lining will be smaller. If the lining was t[he] correct size, machine sew along the line of basting.

10. Insert the lining into your glasses case, tucking in the top edge so th[at] the raw edge does not show. With sewing needle and thread, use the hem[-] ming stitch to sew the lining to the quickpoint stitches around the top [of] the glasses case.

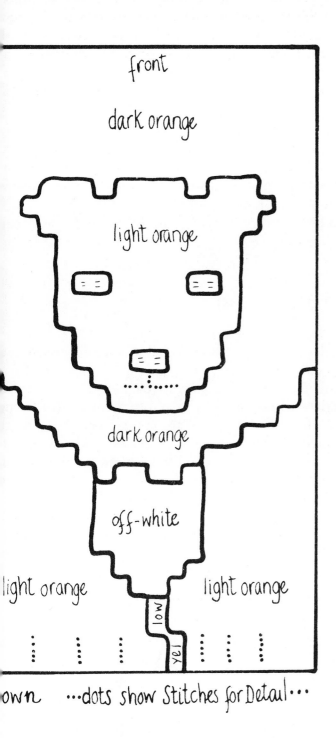

front

dark orange

light orange

dark orange

off-white

light orange   light orange

yel   low

own   ...dots show Stitches for Detail...

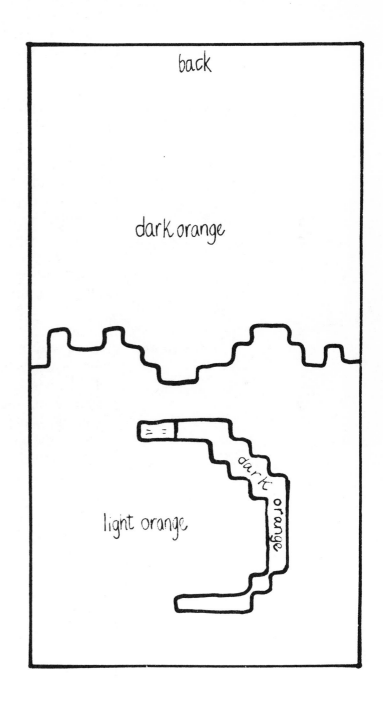

back

dark orange

dark orange

light orange

Geranium Telephone
Book Cover

You can buy a hard-back telephone book cover for your telepho
directory and transform it into a masterpiece. There are two ways to
this: you can glue a piece of quickpoint directly onto a hard-ba
telephone book cover. Or, you can cover the hard-back telephone bo
cover with fabric, then glue on the quickpoint. The latter choice allo
you to select the perfect fabric to complement your quickpoint. The res
is a completely coordinated book cover created by you. Address boo
date books, and loose-leaf notebooks can be decorated in the same wa

You will need: No. 5 quickpoint canvas 12 inches wide by 14 inches long
No. 14 tapestry needle for rug yarn
Yarn in light pink, bright pink, yellow, light green, green, off-white
Hard-back telephone book cover to fit your area's telephone director
(These usually have a metal rod to hold the directory in place and a
available at department stores or office suppliers.)
5/6 yard fabric: 1/2 yard for outside cover, 1/3 yard for inside in matching
correlated color
Scotch tape
White household glue
Clear plastic food wrap

Directions: 1. Trace and paint the design onto the canvas as described on pages 12-
Paint the edge line green.
2. Fold under and baste the margin of canvas (page 14).
3. Quickpoint the design working the flowers and stems first, then the p
Fill in the background after all the shapes are completed.
4. Block the quickpointed canvas.
5. Starting at the lower right-hand corner, whipstitch around the edge li
of the canvas with green yarn.
6. If you have decided to glue your piece of quickpoint directly to t
hard-back telephone book cover, proceed to Step 14. If you are going
cover the telephone book cover with fabric, lay the fabric out flat, wro
side up. Open the telephone book cover and place it in the center of t
fabric so that you are looking at the inside of the cover.

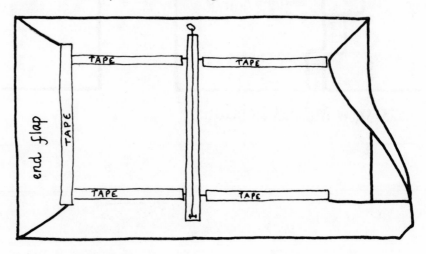

7. Trim the fabric, leaving a three-inch margin on all sides. Trim the corners of the fabric diagonally.

8. Fold the fabric over the top and bottom edges of the book cover and anchor these fabric flaps with scotch tape as shown in the illustration. Fold the end flaps last making neat corners, and then tape in place. Trim the fabric around the metal rod so that the fabric will fit smoothly.

9. Put the directory into the telephone book cover and close the cover. Check to be sure the fabric fits smoothly on the outside of the book cover when it is closed. If the cover will not close completely, loosen the end flaps slightly.

10. You will attach the fabric to the inside of the telephone book cover by applying glue under the fabric flaps gluing the inside of the front cover first, then the inside of the back cover. To insure a good fit, you must glue the fabric in the position that it is taped. Lift the taped edge of the top flap slightly keeping the fabric folded around the book cover. Shoot a line of glue between the flap and the book cover and use your finger to spread a thin, even coat of glue under the flap. Press the flap back in the same position that it was taped. Glue the bottom flap in the same way. Glue the end flap last without letting the fabric shift.

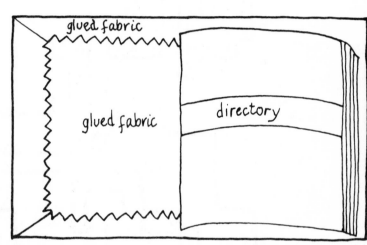

11. Place a piece of clear plastic food wrap over the glued flaps on the inside of the front cover to protect the directory while the glue dries. Close the phone book cover with the directory in it and put books on top to provide even pressure while the glue dries for several hours. This will insure that the fabric will dry without wrinkles.

12. Glue the inside of the back cover in the same way. Before you let the glue dry, look at the closed telephone book cover to see how the fabric fits. If necessary, adjust the end flap quickly before the glue dries. When you are satisfied, place a piece of clear plastic food wrap over the glued flaps and allow the closed phone book cover to dry with books on top.

13. Cover the inside of the book cover with another piece of fabric in the same color as the outside cover or in a correlated color. This fabric will overlap the edges of the glued fabric flaps making the inside of your book cover as neat and colorful as the outside. Cut the piece of fabric so that it will cover the inside of the front cover, overlapping the edges of the fabric flaps. (If you use pinking shears, you will get a nice decorative edge.) Glue the fabric in place. Do the same to the inside of the back cover.

14. Center the piece of quickpoint on the front of the telephone book cover. Spread a thin, even coat of glue on the back of the quickpoint and place the quickpoint on the front of the cover. Place books on top of the quickpoint until the glue dries.

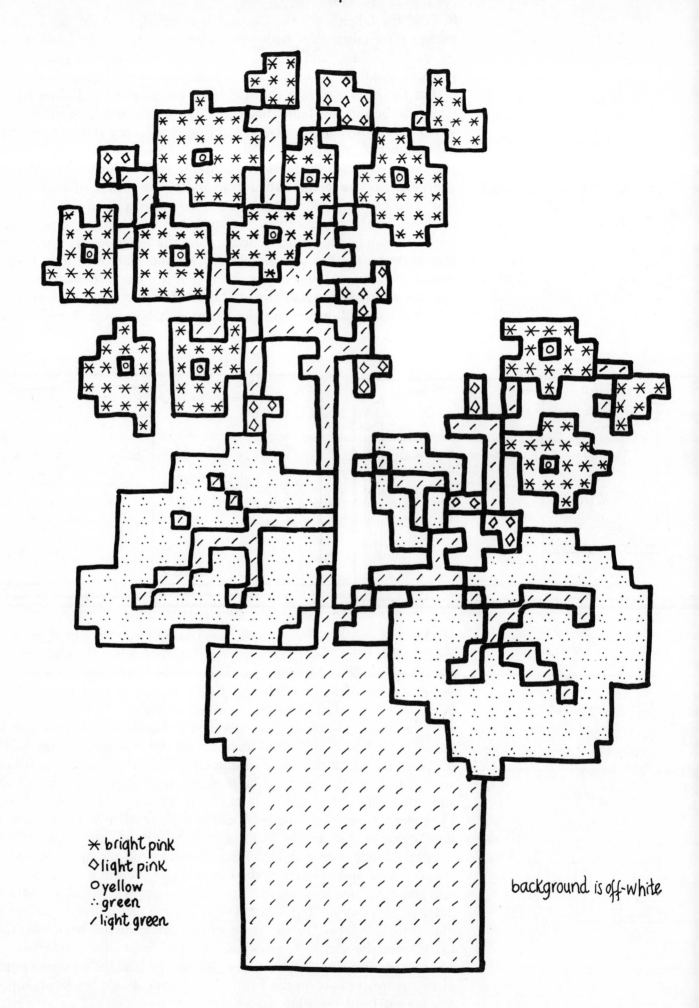

* bright pink
◇ light pink
○ yellow
∴ green
／ light green

background is off-white

42 Geranium Telephone Book Cover

Flower Brick Doorstop or Bookend

A quickpoint-covered brick makes a cheery doorstop for a front hall; two bricks used as bookends will add a splash of color to your bookshelf.

You will need:

No. 5 quickpoint canvas 18 inches wide by 16 inches long
No. 14 tapestry needle for rug yarn
Yarn in white, dark blue, yellow, green, light orange, dark orange
Yellow yarn-for-detail with No. 22 tapestry needle
Brick
Safety pins
Sewing needle and thread
Felt to cover the bottom of the brick, 5 inches by 9 inches

Directions:

1. Trace and paint the design onto the canvas as described on pages 12-13.
2. Fold masking tape over the edges of the canvas (page 10).
3. Quickpoint the design.
4. Block the quickpointed canvas.
5. Stitches for detail: embroider French knots on the dark blue flowers using yellow yarn-for-detail.
6. Lay the quickpointed canvas wrong side up, leaving the masking tape on the edges. Center the brick on top of the quickpointed canvas. Fold the quickpoint around the brick so that the folded corner margins are on the long sides of the brick. This makes a smoother looking brick.
7. Fasten the quickpointed canvas across the corners of the brick with safety pins.
8. Take the brick out of the pinned canvas. With sewing needle and thread sew the quickpoint together at the corners, starting at the top of a corner. Push the sewing needle up through the quickpointed canvas, carry the thread across the corner, and push the needle down through the canvas. Continue to sew down the corner until you reach the margin of canvas. Sew all four corners in this way.
9. Put the brick in the sewn quickpointed canvas. With bottom side up, fold the margins of canvas neatly over the bottom of the brick and hold so that the quickpoint fits snugly around the brick. With quickpoint yarn and needle, make long straight stitches which reach across the bottom. Pull each stitch tightly so that the quickpoint canvas fits snugly around the brick.
10. Cover the margins of canvas on the bottom of the brick with felt. Fold under the edges of the felt as you use the hemming stitch to sew the felt to the quickpoint stitches.

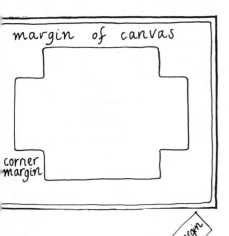

margin of canvas

corner margin

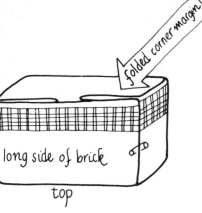

folded corner margin

long side of brick

top

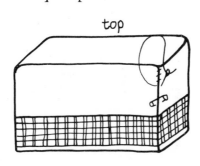

top

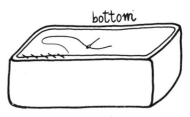

bottom

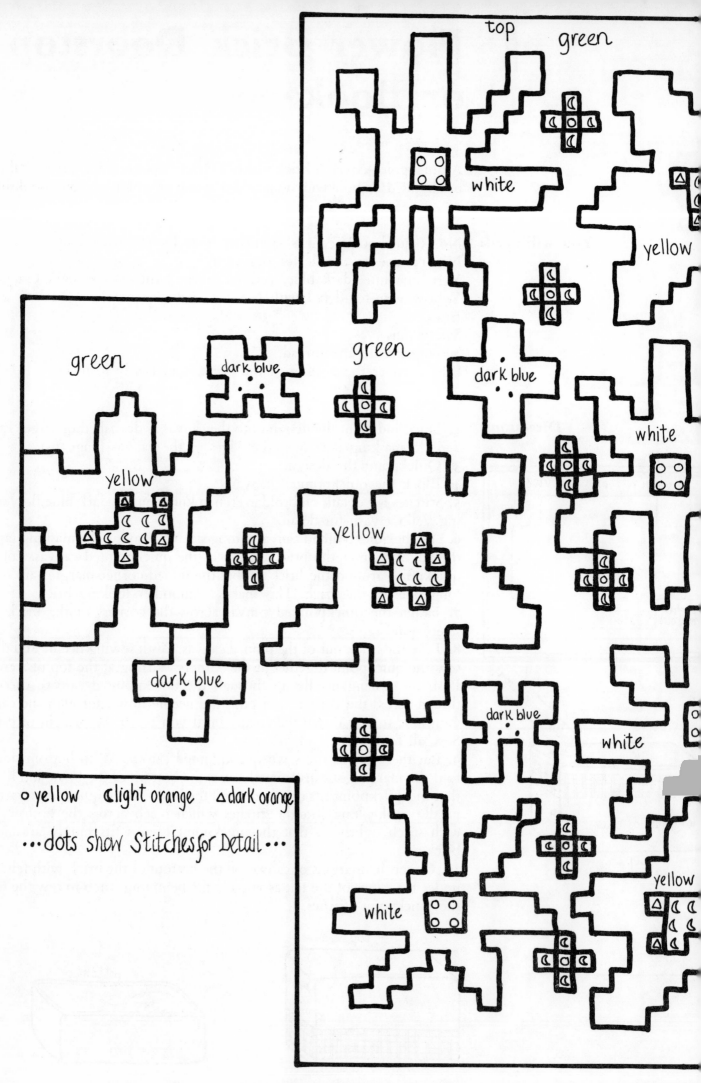

top

green

white

green

dark blue

green

dark blue

yellow

white

yellow

yellow

white

dark blue

yellow

dark blue

white

○ yellow   ☾ light orange   △ dark orange

...dots show Stitches for Detail...

44 Flower Brick Doorstop or Bookend

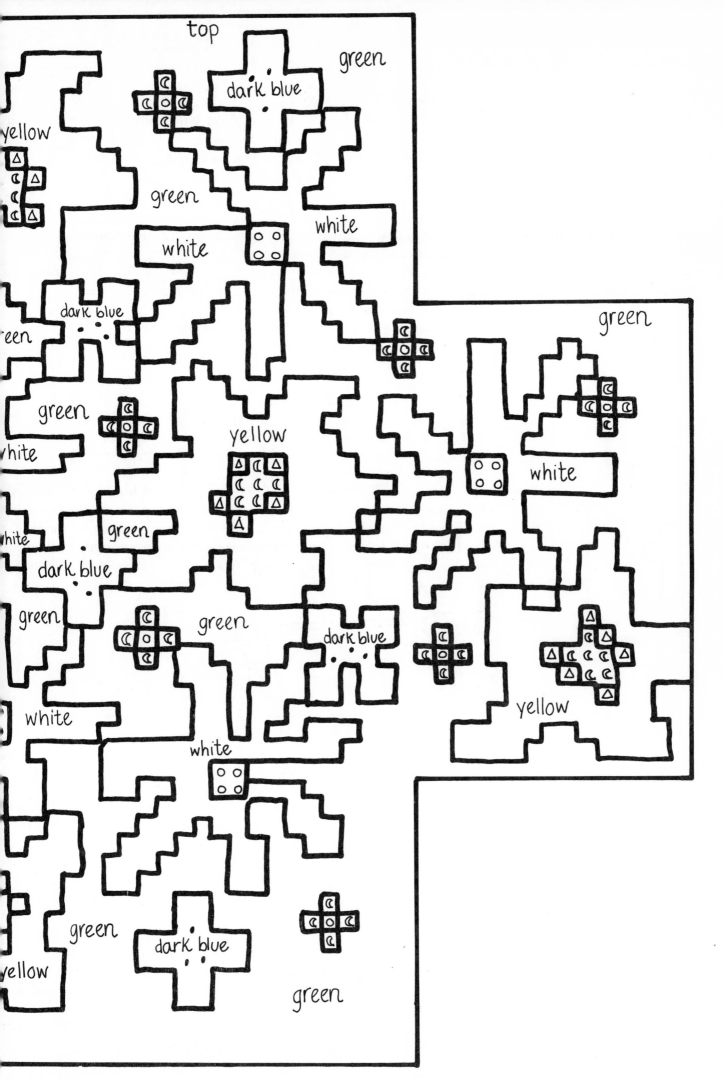

45 Flower Brick Doorstop or Bookend

Green Valley Pencil Case

Any child will love carrying this pencil case. It has a stormy side and sunny side connected by a rainbow. You will enjoy stitching this many colored design. The colors are bright as well as practical and sinc quickpoint is so durable, this pencil case will last for many years. This sam case can also be used as a cosmetic case or travel jewel case.

You will need: No. 5 quickpoint canvas 12 inches wide by 12 inches long
No. 14 tapestry needle for rug yarn
Yarn in light blue, dark blue, yellow, gray, red, orange, blue-green, dar purple, light purple, dark green, green, light green, brown.
Fabric for the lining, 12 inches by 12 inches
9-inch zipper in a color to match or complement the yarn colors
Sewing needle and thread

Directions: 1. Trace and paint the design onto the canvas as described on pages 12-1 tracing trees, rainbow, cloud, and sun first. Paint the edge line dark blu
2. Fold under and baste the margin of canvas (page 14).
3. Quickpoint the design, stitching the smaller shapes first.
4. Block the quickpointed canvas.
5. Fold the pencil case in half with right side out. Whipstitch the two edg lines together with dark blue yarn. Start at the top corner on one side the pencil case and whip down the side to the bottom, joining the front the back. End the yarn. Start another strand of yarn and whipstitch arour the opening; be careful not to stitch your pencil case closed. Continue whip down the other side.

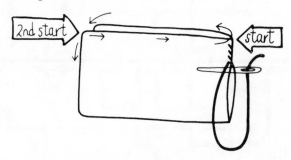

6. Fold the lining fabric in half with right sides together and trim the wid to the same width as that of the pencil case. Baste down the sides 1/2-in from the edge of the fabric. Insert the lining into the pencil case. See how fits; the lining should fit smoothly all around the inside of the case.
7. Remove the basted lining. If the lining was too large, machine se within the line of basting, so that the finished lining will be smaller. If yo lining was the right size, machine sew along the line of basting. Put t lining back into the case, tucking under the top edge so that the raw ed does not show.
8. Close the zipper. Starting at the zipper pull end, tuck one side of t zipper tape between the quickpointed case and the lining. Baste in pla with sewing needle and thread. Tuck in the end of the zipper. Open t zipper and baste the other side in the same way. Close the zipper and adju if necessary. Open the zipper again. Using sewing needle, double threa and a small running stitch, sew in the zipper by hand. You will be sewi through the lining, zipper tape, and quickpointed case.

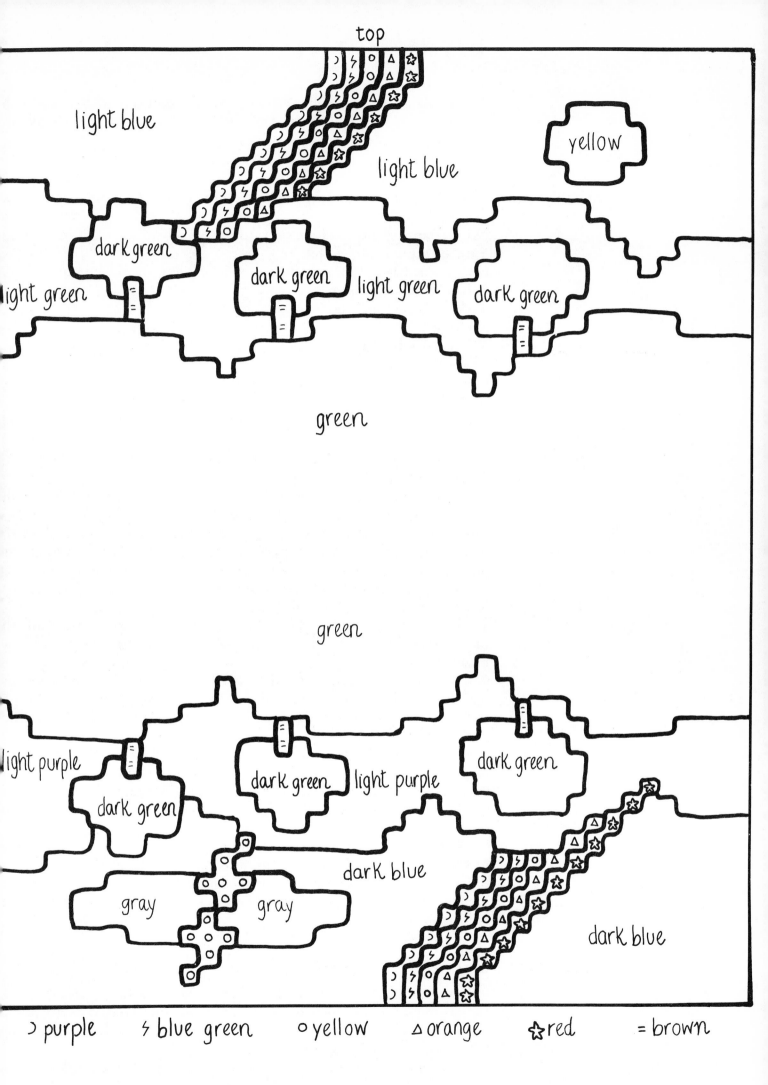

top

light blue

light blue

yellow

dark green

light green

dark green

light green

dark green

green

green

light purple

dark green

dark green

light purple

dark green

gray

gray

dark blue

dark blue

⊃ purple   ϟ blue green   ○ yellow   △ orange   ☆ red   = brown

47 Green Valley Pencil Case

Hobbyhorse

A hobbyhorse is an all-time favorite toy and quickpointed canvas is th perfect material for making it. Any child will love galloping around on hobbyhorse made especially for him.

You will need: Two pieces of no. 5 quickpoint canvas, each 16 inches wide by 18 inche long
No. 14 tapestry needle for rug yarn
Yarn in brown, off-white
One 36-inch length of one-inch dowel or piece of old broom stick
A bag of pillow stuffing
Tacks with 3/8 inch points or staple gun
Masking tape
White household glue
About 1½ yards ribbon
One piece of white felt 4 inches wide by 6 inches long
Buttons for eyes

Directions: 1. Trace the design onto one canvas starting at the top of head (page 50) Tracing instructions are on page 12.
2. For the other side of the hobbyhorse's head, place tracing paper over th design in the book and trace the hobbyhorse's head using a heavy blacl pencil. Turn the tracing paper over. Place the second canvas over th tracing paper and use paint to trace this side of the hobbyhorse's head ont the canvas.
3. Paint the colors of the design onto both canvases (page 13).
4. Fold masking tape over the edges of each canvas (page 10).
5. Work the design on both canvases in Quickpoint stitch or th Interlocking Gobelin stitch. The latter will make the horse look even mor realistic.
6. Block the two quickpointed canvases. If you used the Interlockin Gobelin stitch, your canvases will need extra pulling when you block t make the rows of stitches straight, also firm pinning to hold them in plac as they dry.
7. Machine stay stitch each canvas, sewing through the margin o unworked canvas about 1/4 inch from the worked quickpoint. Machin stay stitch each canvas a second time sewing through the first row o quickpoint stitches along the edge. This line of sewing will keep you canvas from raveling.
8. With right sides together, machine sew the sides of the head together making sure the sides match up and leaving an opening at the bottom fo the dowel and a large opening at the mane for stuffing.
9. Trim the margin of unworked canvas to within 1¼ inch of th quickpointed canvas.
10. Turn the horse's head right side out.
11. Push the dowel through the bottom opening until it touches the top o the head. Put the stuffing through the opening at the mane, distributing th stuffing on either side of the dowel until the head has a nice shape.
12. At the bottom opening, tack or staple the 1¼ inch margin o unworked canvas to the dowel. Cover the tacks or staples with maskin tape.
13. Glue and sew ribbon over the masking tape where the quickpoint an

dowel meet. Tie on additional lengths of ribbon to form reins.

14. Close the opening at the mane with brown quickpoint yarn, using large straight stitches. Stitch straight across the opening, joining the first row of quickpoint stitches on either side. Join corresponding stitches for the length of the mane.

15. For the mane, you will make knots of quickpoint yarn leaving long tails of yarn to resemble horse hair. Thread the needle with a strand of brown yarn and a strand of white yarn. Starting at the bottom of the seam of straight stitches, push the needle down and up through the worked quickpoint, leaving a three-inch tail. Knot the yarn at the quickpoint and cut the yarn off at three inches. Make the mane three knots wide: do one knot on each side of the straight stitch seam and make the third knot on the seam. Do a few extra knots between the ears to form the forelock. Trim all the tails of yarn until the mane looks right.

16. To make the ears, cut two triangles of white felt 2 inches wide by 3 inches wide. Fold each ear in half with point up. With sewing needle and thread, use the straight stitch to sew the folded ears on the hobbyhorse with the opening of the ear toward the front.

17. Sew on two buttons for eyes.

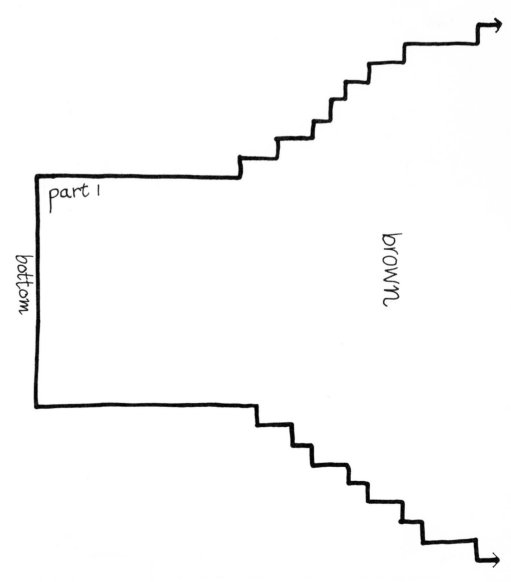

part 1

bottom

brown

49 Hobbyhorse (bottom)

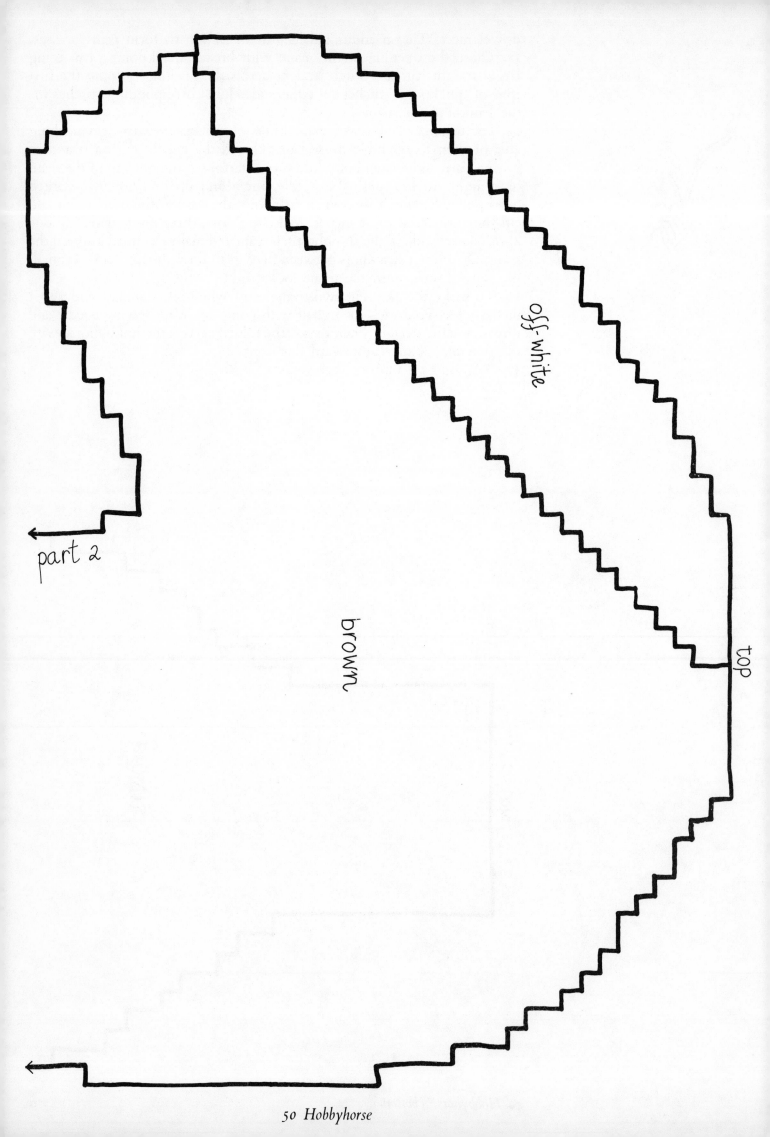

part 2

off-white

brown

top

Dirndl Doll

The Dirndl Doll has a front and back design. It is a perfect gift for a grandmother to stitch for her granddaughter. This doll is an adorable pillow and a wonderful toy.

You will need: Two pieces of No. 5 quickpoint canvas, each 14 inches wide and 18 inches long
No. 14 tapestry needle for rug yarn
Yarn in green, yellow, dark blue, red, off-white, pink, orange, light blue
A bag of pillow stuffing
Sewing needle and thread

Directions: 1. Trace and paint the design onto the canvas as described on pages 12-13, tracing the face and flowers first.
2. Fold masking tape over the edges of the canvas (page 10).
3. Quickpoint the front of the doll, stitching the face and flowers first. Quickpoint the back of the doll.
4. Block the quickpointed canvases.
5. Machine stay stitch each canvas, sewing through the margin of unworked canvas about 1/4-inch from the worked quickpoint. Machine stay stitch each canvas a second time, sewing through the first row of quickpoint stitches along the edge. This line of sewing will keep your canvas from raveling.
6. With right sides together, line up the design and baste the front to the back with sewing needle and thread.
7. Machine sew the front to the back, keeping your sewing lines as close to the edge of the worked quickpoint as you can. Leave an opening across the bottom for stuffing.
8. Trim the margin of unworked canvas to within 1 1/4 inch of the quickpointed design on both the front and back of the doll.
9. Turn the doll right side out and fill with pillow stuffing.
10. With sewing needle and thread, sew the doll closed using the hemming stitch.

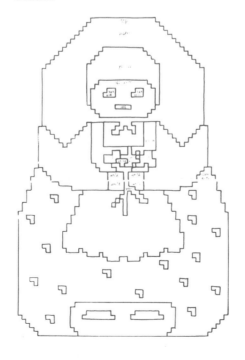
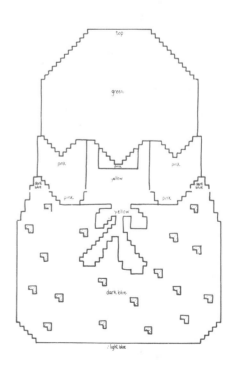

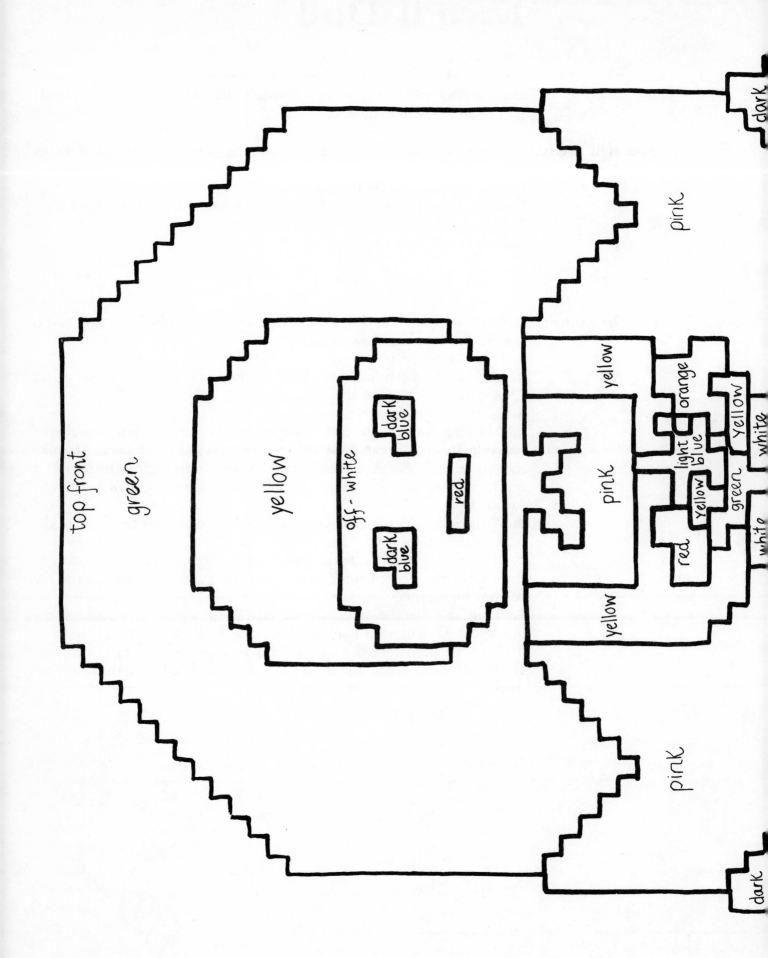

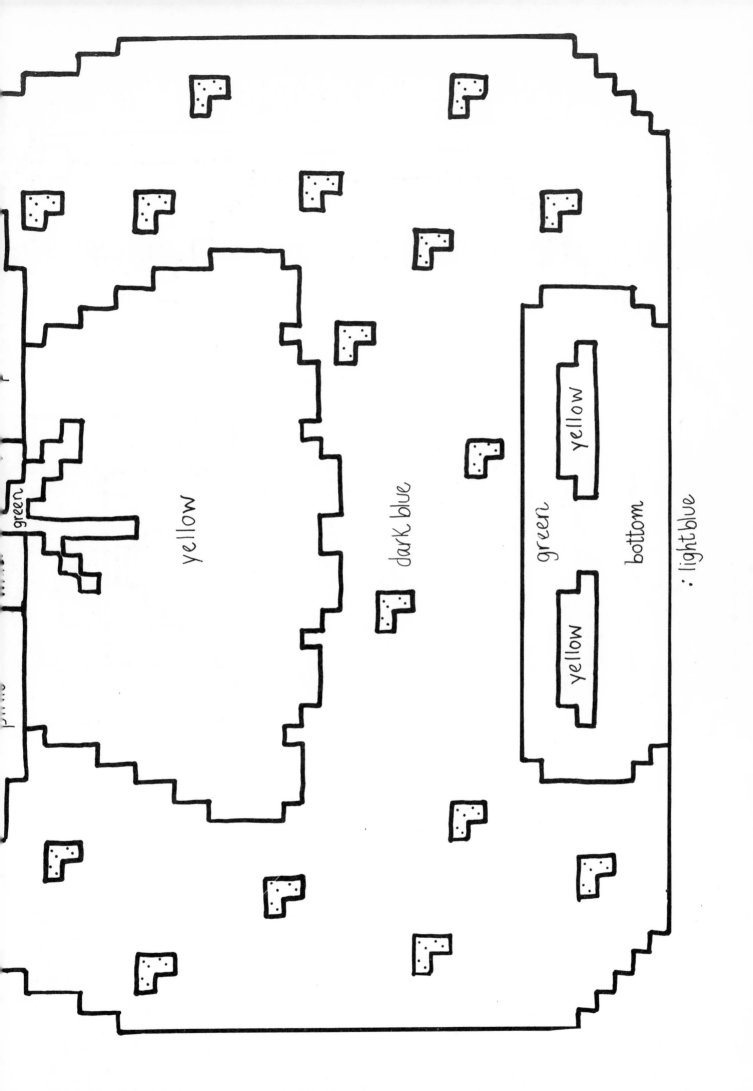

green

yellow

dark blue

green

yellow

yellow

bottom

: light blue

53 Dirndl Doll (front)

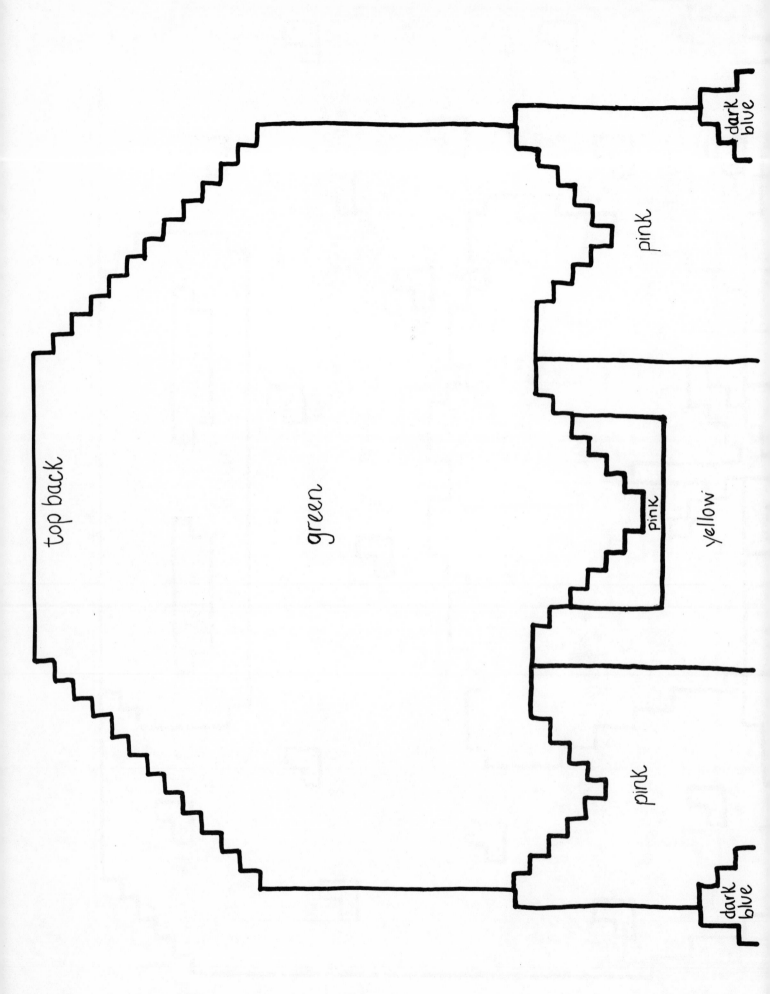

green

top back

pink

pink

yellow

pink

dark blue

dark blue

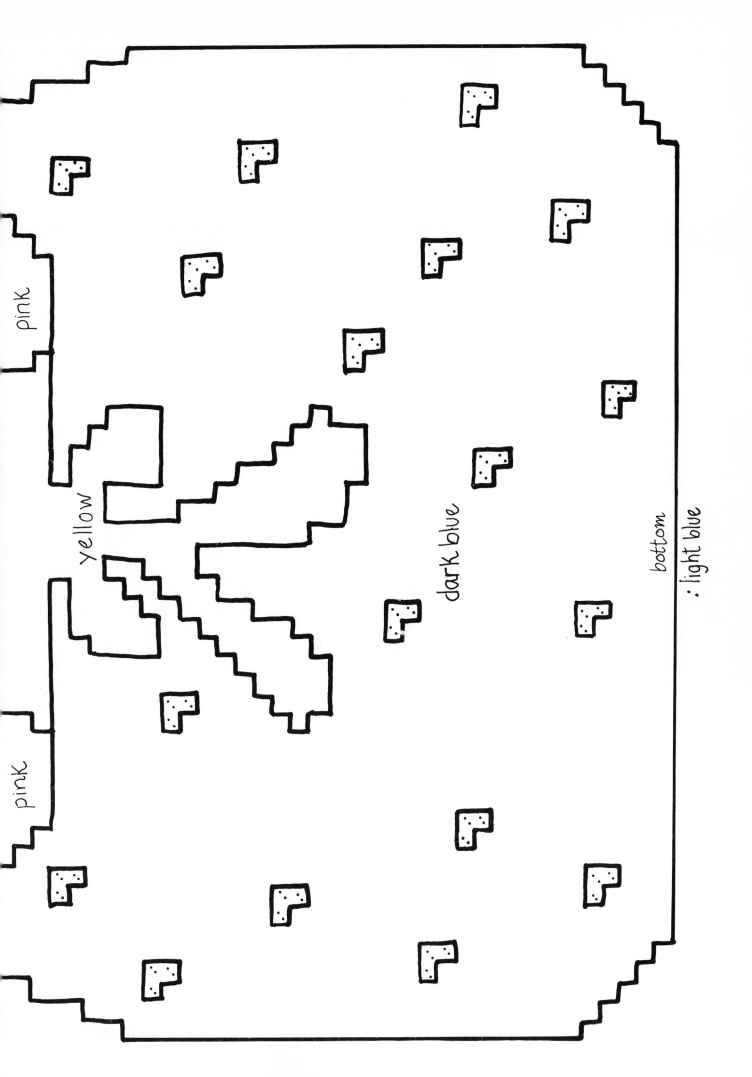

pink

pink

yellow

dark blue

bottom

: light blue

55 Dirndl Doll (back)

Envelope Handbag

Why not stitch the ultimate in an envelope handbag—one that looks like [a] mailing envelope! You can make a quickpoint handbag that looks like [a] manilla-colored envelope or one that matches the colors of your person[al] stationery.

Quickpoint a stamp on the front, back stitch your initials, add a strap [if] you want to; now you are ready to go!

For those who prefer a roomier handbag, a larger outline is also on th[e] design. You will find more ideas for the envelope and other handbags o[n] the pages which follow and in Creating Your Own Projects.

You will need:
No. 5 quickpoint canvas 12½ inches wide by 22 inches long
No. 14 tapestry needle for rug yarn
Yarn in light blue or beige for the envelope, dark blue or green for th[e] accent lines and edge stitches, red, white, and blue for the stamp
Blue or green yarn-for-detail with No. 22 tapestry needle
1/3-yard of fabric in calico print or corduroy for lining
Straight pins
Sewing needle and white thread, and thread to match the fabric
Poster board or blotter paper, 12 inches wide by 24 inches long
Safety pins
Snap (optional)
A yard of ribbon or a chain belt (optional)

Directions:
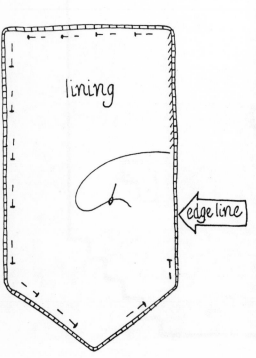

1. Trace and paint the design onto the canvas as described on pages 12-13.
2. Fold under and baste the margin of canvas (page 14). Fold and baste th[e] flap carefully. Trim the point of the flap straight across to within thre[e] squares of the edge line. The squares on the edge line of the painted fla[p] will align diagonally.
3. Quickpoint the canvas.
4. Block the quickpointed canvas.
5. Stitches for detail: with yarn-for-detail in your accent color, use th[e] back stitch to embroider your initials on the center front of the envelop[e.] Copy your monogram from your stationery or create your own b[y] copying initials from a lettering alphabet. With sewing needle and whit[e] thread, put French knots on the blue area of the flag stamp to make stars.
6. Either poster board or blotter will give your handbag the crisp, custo[m] look you desire. Poster board makes a stiffer handbag than blotter pape[r] but both materials will provide adequate stiffness. Trim the width of th[e] poster board or blotter to measure 1/2-inch less than the width of th[e] quickpointed canvas. Trim the length of the poster board to measure 1 1[/2] inches less than the length of the blocked canvas. This will give the post[er] board room to shift when you fold over the flap of your handbag.
7. Lay the quickpointed canvas right side down, place the poster board o[n] top of the canvas and the lining fabric right side up on top of the post[er] board. Trim the lining so that it is one inch bigger than the canvas on a[ll] sides.
8. Tuck the edges of the lining under the poster board and pin the lining t[o] the row of quickpoint stitches nearest the edge line.
9. Fold the handbag so that the flap overlaps the front. If the lining pee[ls] out from under the flap, re-pin the lining so that the lining does not sho[w] when the handbag is folded.

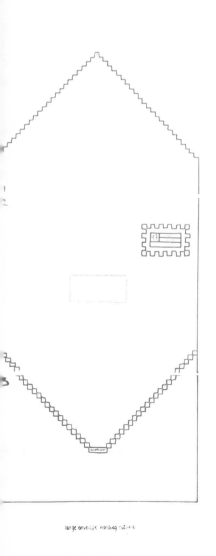

10. Unfold the handbag. With sewing needle and thread sew the lining to the quickpoint stitches nearest the edge lines with the hemming stitch. The poster board lies between the lining and the quickpointed canvas; do *not* sew through the poster board.

11. Fold the flap over again. To form the bottom of the handbag, crease along one row of worked quickpoint stitches. The crease should be straight and crisp. Put safety pins through the squares of canvas on the edge lines at either end of the crease.

12. With the binding stitch (pages 22-23) join the front of the handbag to the back along the edge lines using your accent color yarn. Start at the pin at the crease on the right-hand side of your handbag and do the binding stitch up the right-hand side of your handbag. Continue to do the binding stitch on the edge line of the flap. Stop at the center point of the flap. You will be stitching along a diagonal edge line on the flap. This is somewhat more difficult than working on the straight edge line, so be especially careful in placing your stitches.

13. Starting at the pin on the opposite side, do the binding stitch up the left-hand side. Continue to do the binding stitch on the edge line of the flap until you reach the center point.

14. Do the binding stitch on the top edge line of the front.

15. For additional security, sew a snap to the inside of the flap and to the front of your handbag.

16. If you decide to add a strap, make one with ribbon or use a chain belt for an attractive and sturdy strap. You can adjust the length of the ribbon or chain belt to make a short handle or a shoulder length strap. Tuck the ends of the strap inside the handbag between the front and the back at the top corners. With sewing needle and double thread, hand sew the strap to the top corners where the front and the back meet.

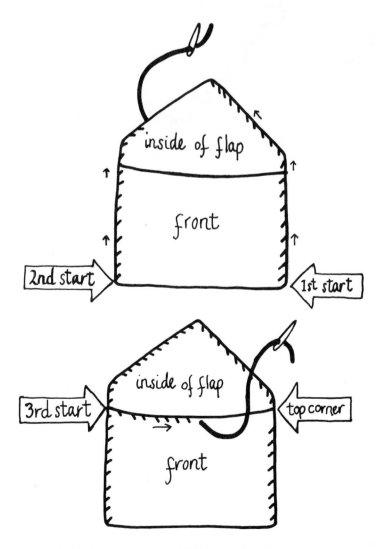

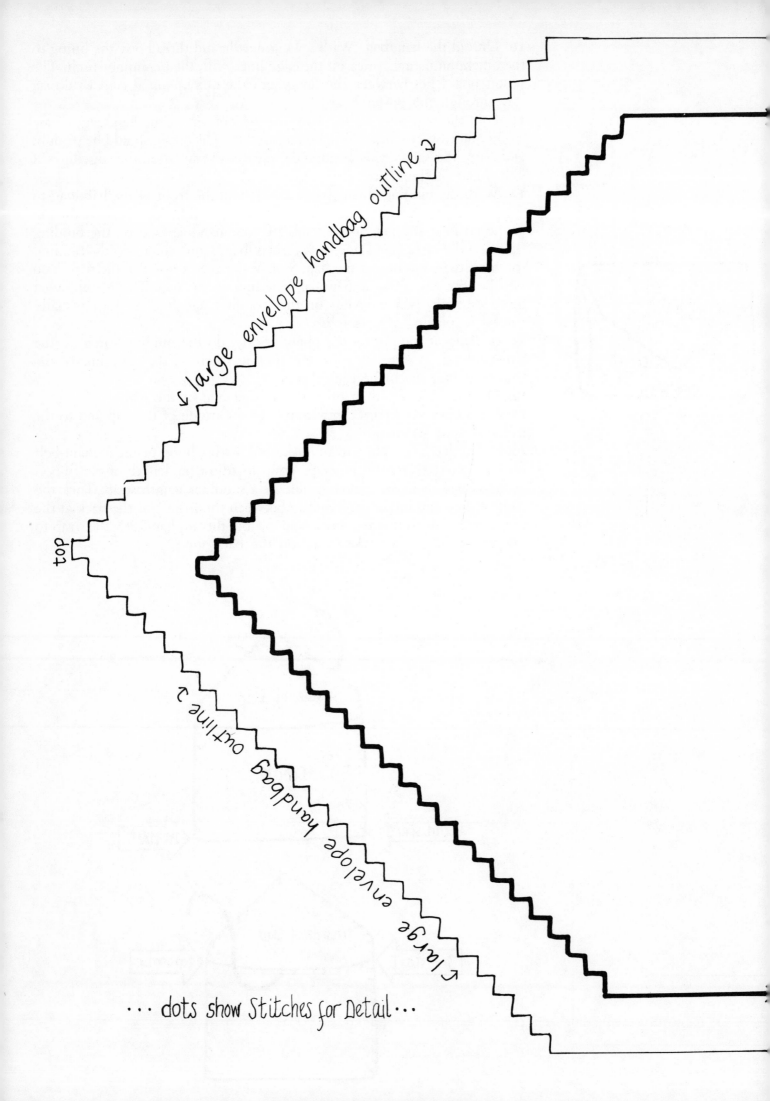

‹ large envelope handbag outline ›

top

‹ large envelope handbag outline ›

··· dots show Stitches for Detail ···

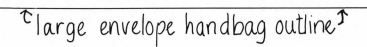

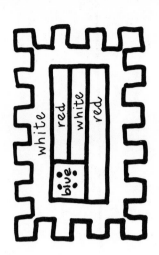

initials

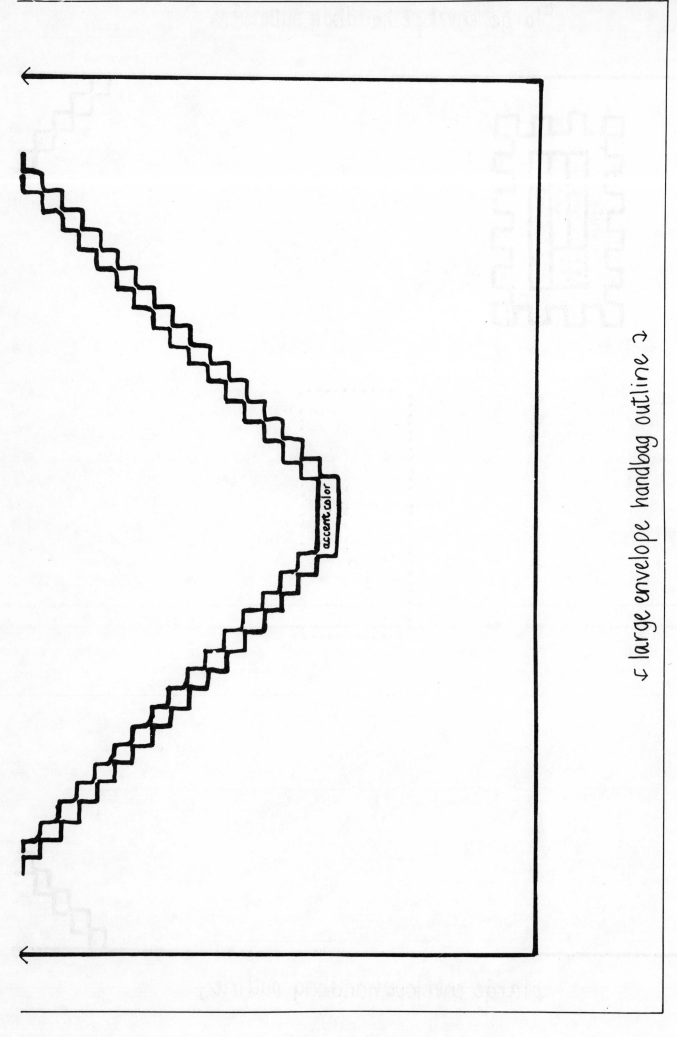

← large envelope handbag outline ↗

accent color

Picture Frames

Your favorite photograph will never look better than in a quickpoint picture frame. You'll want to stitch more than one because these picture frames look fabulous when grouped on a table top.

You will need:

No. 5 quickpoint canvas 12 inches wide by 14 inches long
No. 14 tapestry needle for rug yarn
Bunny design: yarn in light blue, beige, white, green, and orange
Tulip design: yarn in yellow, light blue, and green
8 by 10-inch standing plexiglass picture frame
Tube of clear household cement
Colored paper

Directions:

1. Trace and paint the design onto the canvas as described on pages 12-13. Paint the edge lines of each design green. On the *Tulip* design, paint two lines of canvas around the design green. (The outer one is the edge line.)
2. Fold under and baste the margin of canvas (page 14).

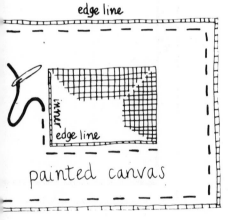

painted canvas

3. To create a margin of canvas in the center cut out a square in the center of the canvas five squares from the *inner* edge line of the design. Snip cautiously from the corners of this opening toward the corners of the inner edge line of the design. Do not snip the inner edge line. Fold under and baste this margin of canvas (page 14).
4. Quickpoint the design.
5. Block the quickpointed canvas. The threads of canvas are short at the corners of the inner edge line. Do not worry; these will be covered by the binding stitch. Do not place pins at the corners of the inner edge line.
6. Stitches for detail: on the *Bunny* design, use white quickpoint yarn to embroider each bunny's tail with a French knot. Use green quickpoint yarn and three straight stitches to make the carrot tops and clumps of grass.
7. Starting at the upper right-hand corner, do the binding stitch (pages 22-23) all the way around the outer edge line of the picture frame with green yarn.
8. Start at the upper left-hand corner of the center opening and do the binding stitch all the way around the opening.
9. Spread a thin, even coat of clear household cement on the back of the quickpointed canvas.

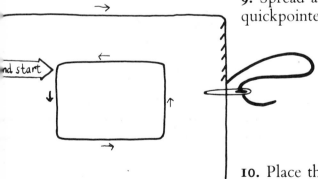

10. Place the canvas on the picture frame so that the bottom edge of the quickpoint aligns with the bottom edge of the picture frame and the other three sides cover the plexiglass. Lay the picture frame on the edge of a table with quickpoint side up. Place books on top of the picture frame to provide even pressure while the glue dries. Leave overnight.
11. Put the photograph into the picture frame. For a finishing touch, place a piece of colored paper behind the photograph so your frame will look attractive from the back, too.

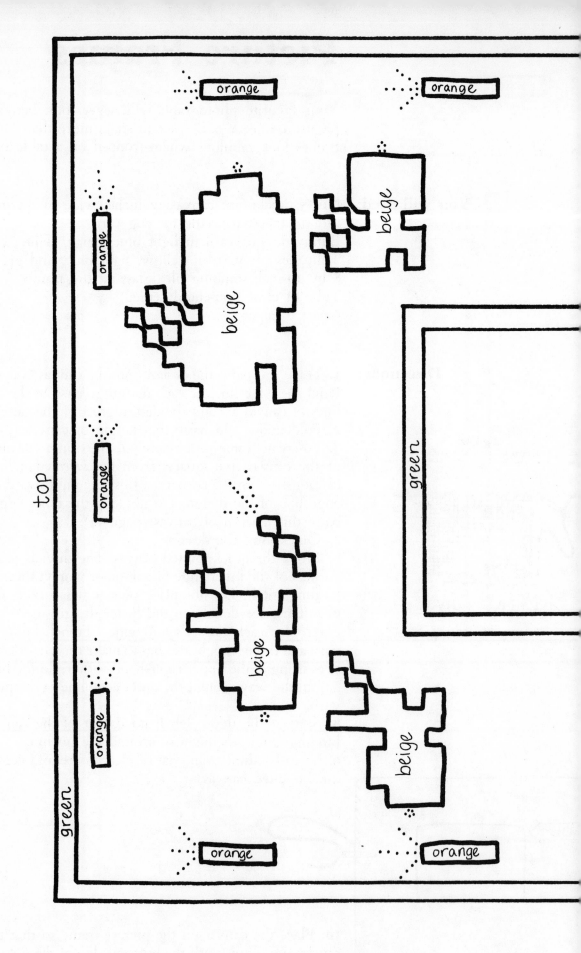

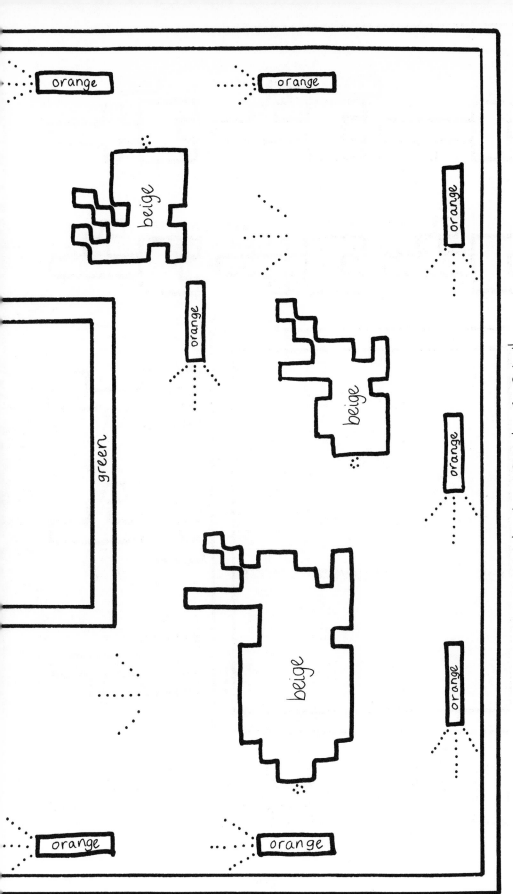

orange orange

beige

orange

beige

green

orange

beige

orange

orange orange

·····dots show Stitches for Detail·····

63 Bunny Design Picture Frame

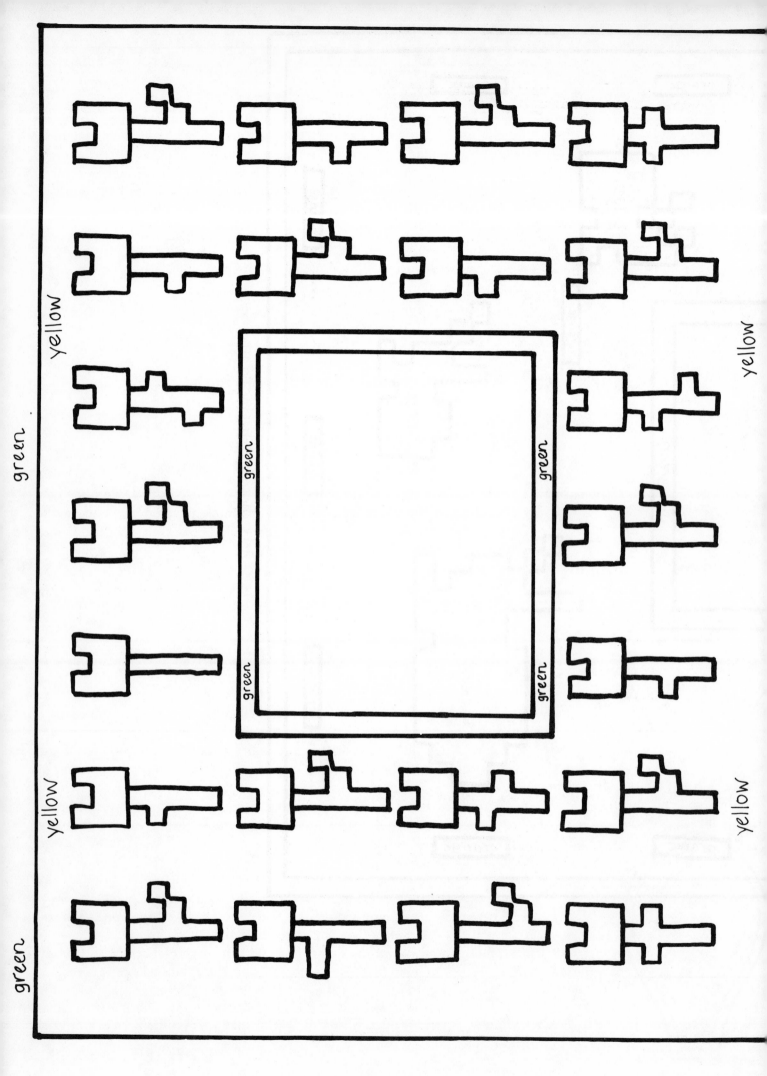

64 Tulip Design Picture Frame

Tennis Racquet Cover

The best way we've found to keep a racquet dry and beautiful is to sew a quickpointed canvas to a vinyl tennis racquet cover. Your racquet will be waterproof and even if you lose a set, you'll still enjoy carrying your racquet in its cheerful quickpoint cover. Before you start this project, buy a vinyl tennis racquet cover that fits your racquet. You will be working your design to fit the cover.

You will need:
No. 5 quickpoint canvas 24 inches wide by 29 inches long
No. 14 tapestry needle for rug yarn
Yarn in dark blue, light blue, yellow, bright pink, dark orange, light orange, green, blue-green, red
Vinyl tennis racquet cover to fit your racquet and look attractive with the design colors
Foldover braid, one package or two yards of braid in a correlating color
Sewing needle and thread
Straight pins
White household glue

Directions:

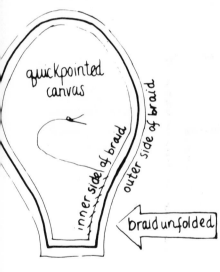

1. Place your vinyl tennis racquet cover on top of your canvas and trace the outline of the cover onto the canvas with a pencil. This will be the outline. Put the canvas over the design in the book, centering the design within the outline. Trace and paint the design onto the canvas as described on pages 12-13.
2. Fold masking tape over the edges of the canvas (page 10).
3. Quickpoint the design, working the three leaf shapes first, then filling in the squares.
4. Block the quickpointed canvas.
5. Machine stay stitch through the margin of unworked canvas about 1/4-inch from the worked quickpoint. This will keep your canvas from raveling.
6. Trim the margin of unworked canvas to within 1 1/4 inch of the worked quickpoint.
7. Fold the margin of unworked canvas under the worked quickpoint and steam iron around the edge of the canvas. This makes the canvas easier to work on.
8. Unfold the braid. Starting at the narrow end of the quickpoint canvas, arrange the braid around the canvas placing the middle crease of the braid on the edge of the canvas. Pin the inner side of the braid to the quickpointed canvas.
9. With the hemming stitch, hand sew the inner side of the braid to the quickpointed canvas, leaving the outer side of the braid unattached.
10. Place the quickpointed canvas on the vinyl cover and fold the unattached outer side of the braid around the vinyl cover.
11. Hand sew through the layers of braid, canvas, vinyl cover and braid. (A large running stitch looks great with the chunky quickpoint stitches.)
12. When you have sewn three-quarters of the way around, apply glue evenly between the canvas and the vinyl cover. To insure that the canvas will dry smoothly, place books on top of the quickpointed cover until the glue dries. Finish sewing when glued surfaces are completely dry.

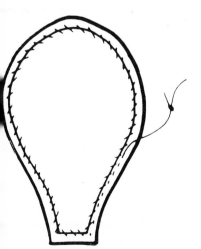

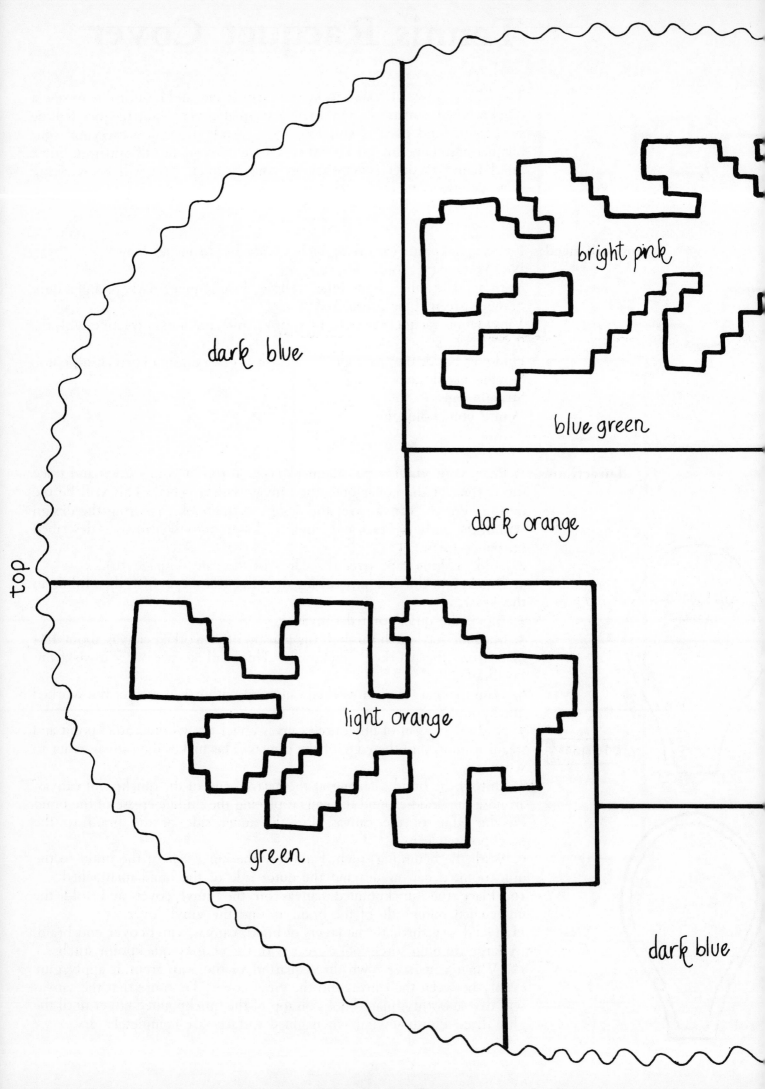

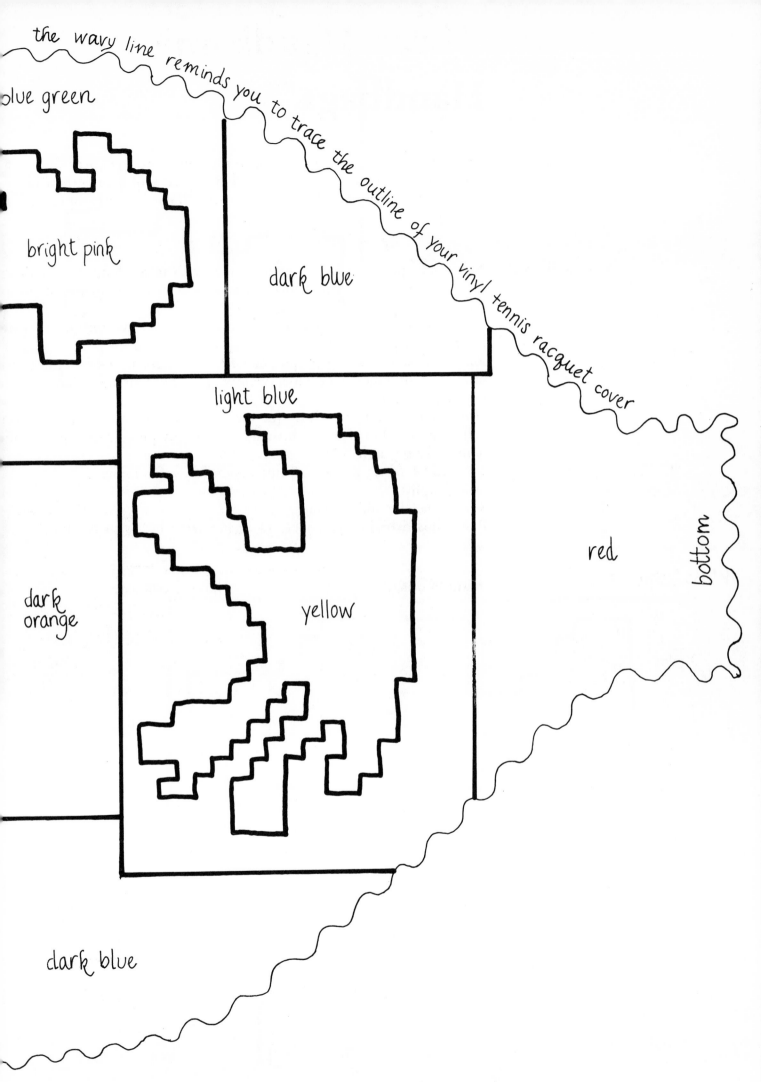

the wavy line reminds you to trace the outline of your vinyl tennis racquet cover

blue green

bright pink

dark blue

light blue

dark orange

yellow

red

bottom

dark blue

67 Tennis Racquet Cover

Three Handsome Handbags

Since you always have a handbag with you, why not carry one that uniquely your own? Here are three designs that will help you create eye catching handbags durable enough to carry all day, yet elegant enough for evening.

You will need: No. 5 quickpoint canvas, 14 inches wide by 28 inches long (for handbag
No. 5 quickpoint canvas, 5 inches wide by 38 inches long (for the strap
No. 14 tapestry needle for rug yarn
Matisse design: yarn in blue, pale blue, orange, yellow, turquoise, white
bright pink, green, blue-green
Rainbow design: yarn in purple, lavender, dark green, green, light green
brown, light blue, dark blue, yellow, red, light orange, dark orange
bright pink, white
House design: yarn in yellow (or the color of your house), gray, green
yellow-green, light green, brown, red, bright pink, dark blue, white
orange, beige, light blue
1/3 yard of fabric in calico print or corduroy for lining
Straight pins
Sewing needle and thread
Poster board or blotter paper, 12 inches wide by 24 inches long

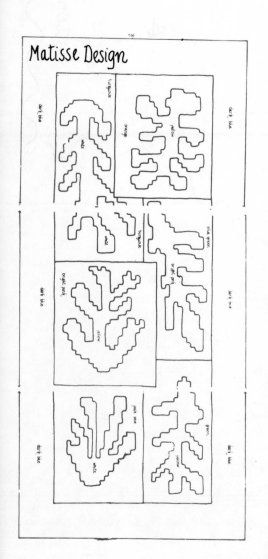

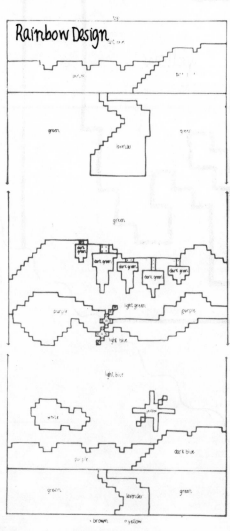

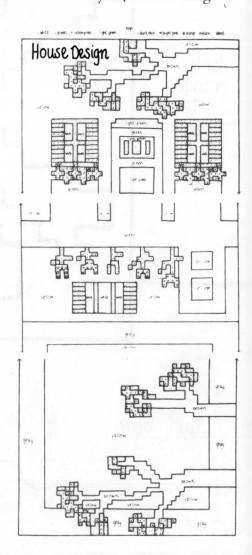

Directions:

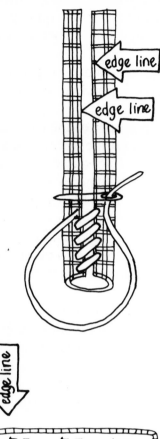

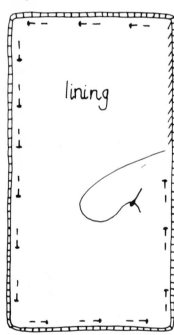

1. Trace, and paint the design onto the handbag canvas as described on pages 12-13. Trace the strap outline onto the canvas in sections following the numbered steps on pages 80-81. Be sure the outlines meet to make a continuous strap outline.

For the *Matisse* handbag's strap, paint the canvas within the outline dark blue.

For the *Rainbow* handbag's strap, paint stripes of color one crossing wide for the length of the strap. Paint the stripes in this order: red, orange, light orange, yellow, green, dark blue, purple, bright pink, red, orange, light orange, yellow, green, dark blue, purple, bright pink.

For the *House* handbag's strap, trace the outline and the lines of the strap design in sections, then paint in the colors as listed on the design.

2. Fold under and baste the margin of the handbag canvas (page 14). Fold under and baste the margin of canvas of the strap.

3. Quickpoint the canvas for the handbag.

4. Before quickpointing the strap, whipstitch the two edge lines together for the *length* of the canvas that will be the strap. (This is the only time in the book that you whipstitch *before* you quickpoint). Flatten the strap so that the seam of whipstitches goes down the center of the strap. This will be the underside of the strap. Quickpoint this side first working down the length of the strap. Turn the strap over and quickpoint this side of the strap, pressing the two sides together as you stitch. To make a neat, flat strap rather than a hollow tube, every fifth stitch or so try to catch some yarn (from the backs of the quickpoint stitches on the other side of the strap) with your needle as you make your quickpoint stitch. You will feel that you have caught the backs of the stitches that are within the strap as you pull your needle through to complete the stitch. This holds the two sides of the strap firmly together. When you have quickpointed the entire strap, steam iron it but do not block.

5. Block the quickpointed canvas for the handbag.

6. Either poster board or blotter will give your handbag the crisp custom look you desire. Poster board makes a stiffer handbag than blotter paper, but both materials will provide adequate stiffness. Trim the width of the poster board or blotter to measure 1/2 inch less than the width of the quickpointed handbag canvas. Trim the length of the board or blotter to measure 1½ inches less than the length of the canvas. This will give the board or blotter room to shift when you fold over the flap of your handbag.

7. Lay the quickpointed handbag canvas right side down. Place the poster board on top of the canvas and place the lining right side up on top of the poster board. Trim the lining so that it is one inch larger than the canvas on all sides.

8. Tuck the edges of the lining under the poster board and pin the lining to the row of quickpoint stitches nearest the edge line.

9. Fold the handbag so that the flap overlaps the front. If the lining peeks out from under the flap, re-pin the lining so that the lining does not show when the handbag is folded.

10. Unfold the handbag and use the hemming stitch to sew the lining to the quickpoint stitches nearest the edge lines. The poster board lies between the lining and the quickpointed canvas; do *not* sew through the poster board.

11. Fold the flap over again, lining up the design on the flap with the design on the front of the handbag.

12. With the flap still folded over the front, decide where you want to crease the front to form the bottom of the handbag. Flatten across this line using one row of worked quickpoint stitches as your guide in forming a straight, crisp crease.

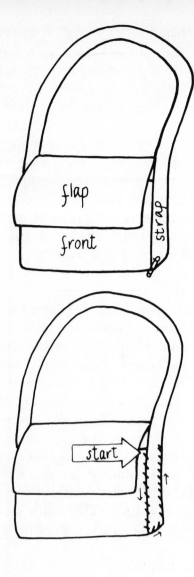

13. On the right-hand side, pin the corner of the strap to the front crease a the edge line. Pin the corner of the other end of the strap to the front crea on the left-hand side. Make sure the strap is not twisted and that the rig side of the strap is facing out. When you do the binding stitch (pages 2: 23) to join your handbag pieces together, you are doing something new you are joining the edge lines of the handbag to the quickpointed stra with every binding stitch. Match each edge line square to a quickpoi stitch as you work.

14. On the right-hand side, hold the strap and handbag together so that th quickpointed stitches on the strap match corresponding squares on the edg line.

15. On the right hand side, start at the top corner of the front and bindin stitch the strap to the handbag, working down the front. Use a color yar that complements your handbag or change colors as you work to matc the design. As you make your stitches, catch some of the lines of canv from the strap in your stitches. Bind the bottom of the strap to the handba to form the bottom. Bind up the back of the handbag until you are eve with the top front corner. Do an extra binding stitch and end off the yar

16. On the left-hand side, binding stitch the handbag to the strap starting the top corner, proceeding down the front, around the bottom, and up th back until you are even with the (left) top corner. (To insure that the sid of your handbag will match, be sure the number of stitches on your stra from pin to top corner on the left-hand side equal the number of stitches c the side that is binding stitched.) Do an extra binding stitch and contin to binding stitch around the edge line of the flap. When you have bindir stitched completely around the flap, end off the yarn.

17. Complete your handbag by doing the binding stitch across the top edg line of the front.

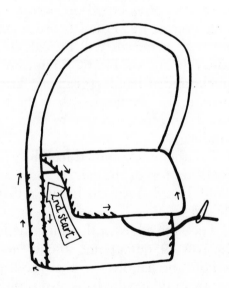 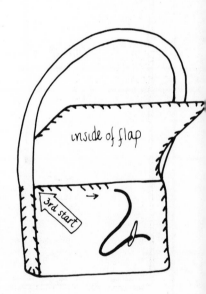

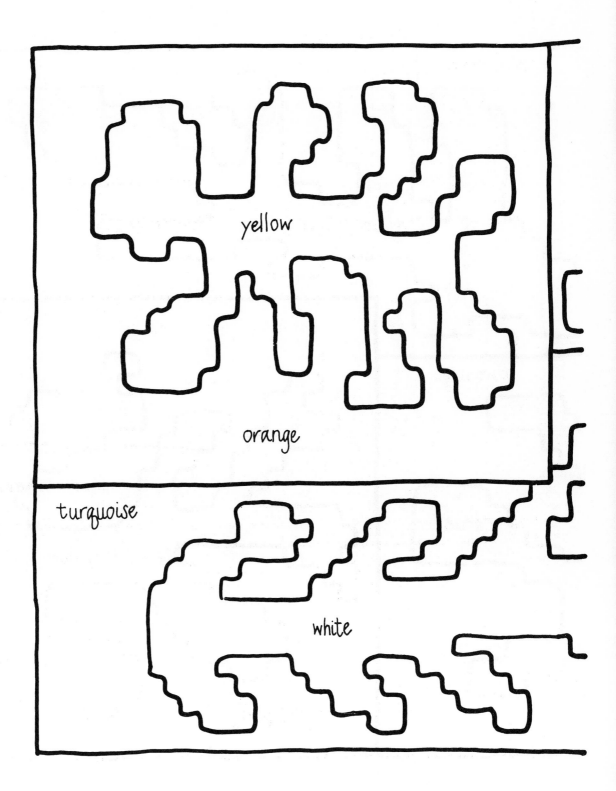

dark blue

top

yellow

orange

turquoise

white

dark blue

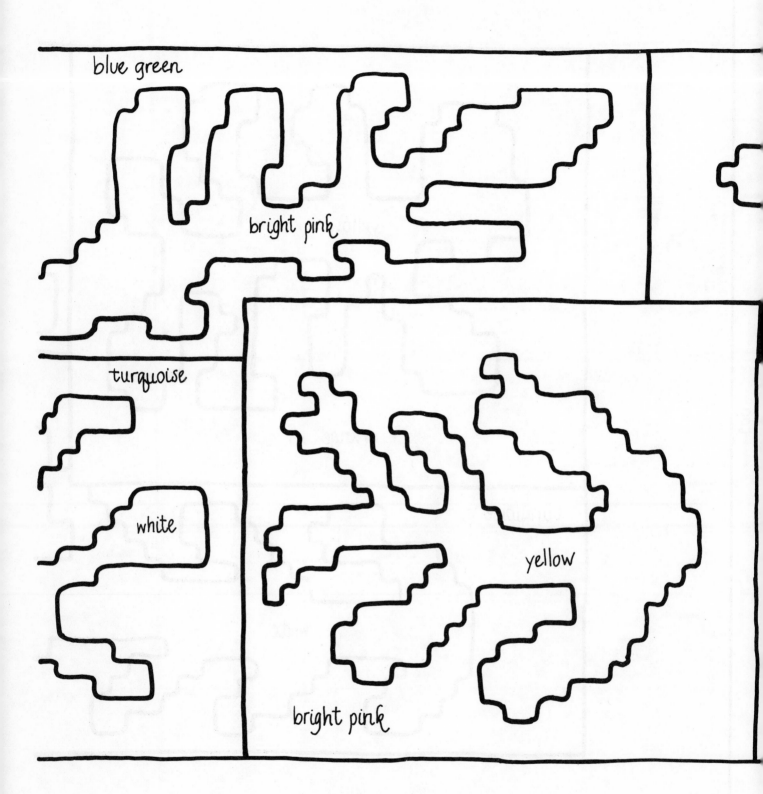

dark blue

blue green

bright pink

turquoise

white

yellow

bright pink

dark blue

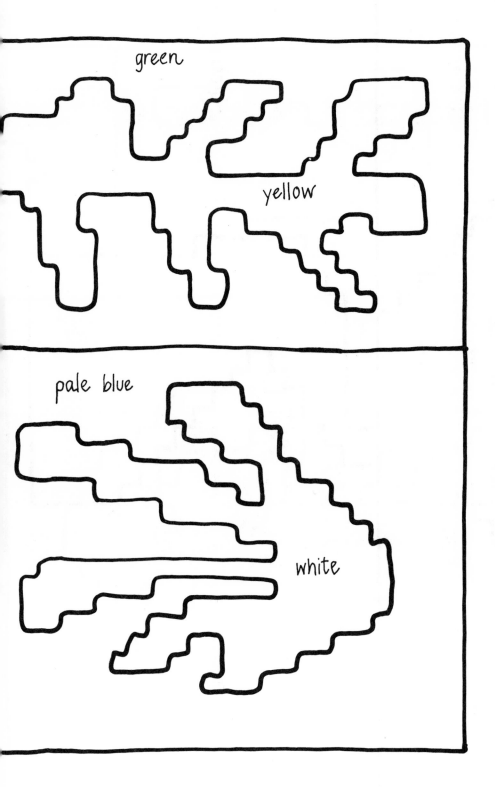

dark blue

green

yellow

pale blue

white

dark blue

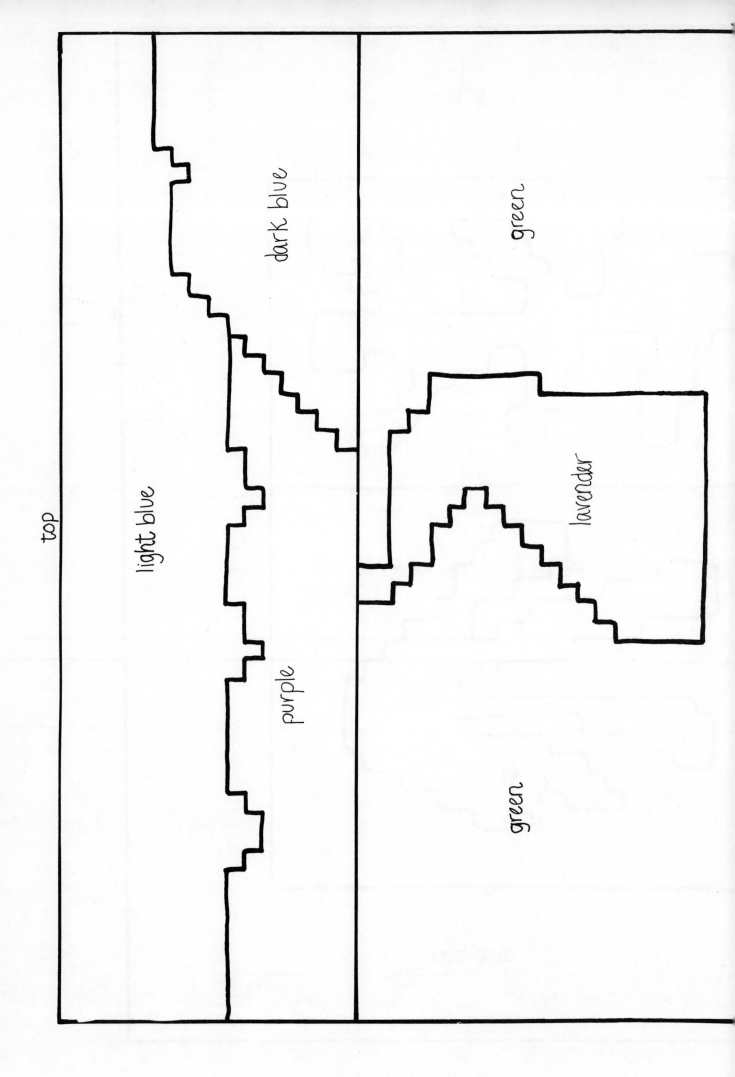

top

light blue

dark blue

purple

green

lavender

green

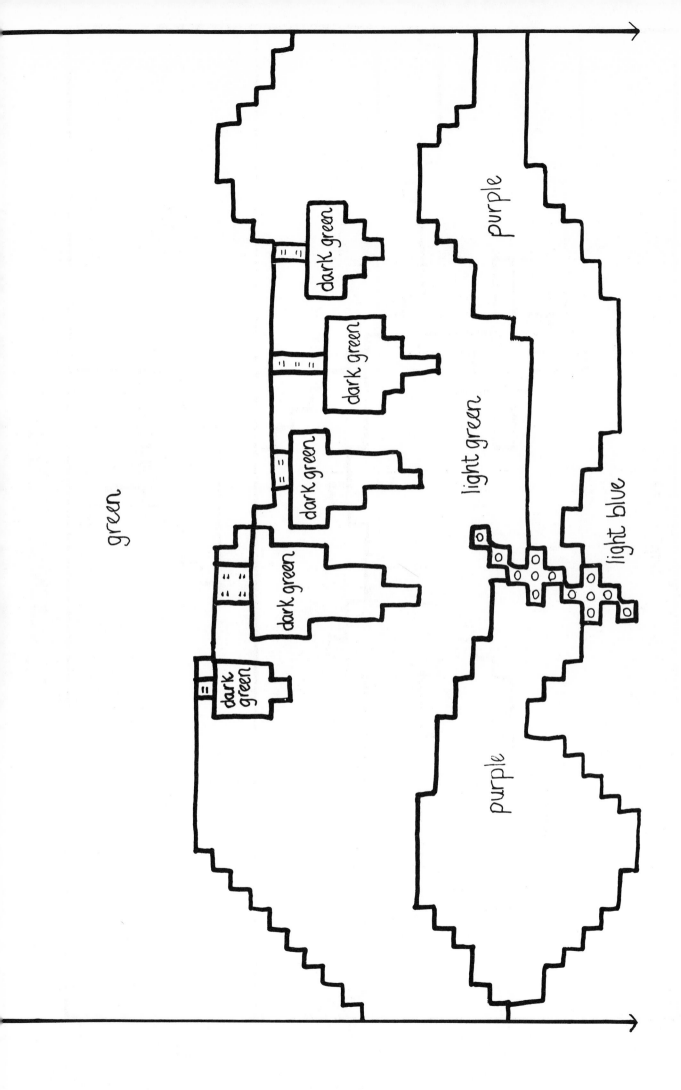

green

dark green

dark green

dark green

dark green

dark green

purple

light green

light blue

purple

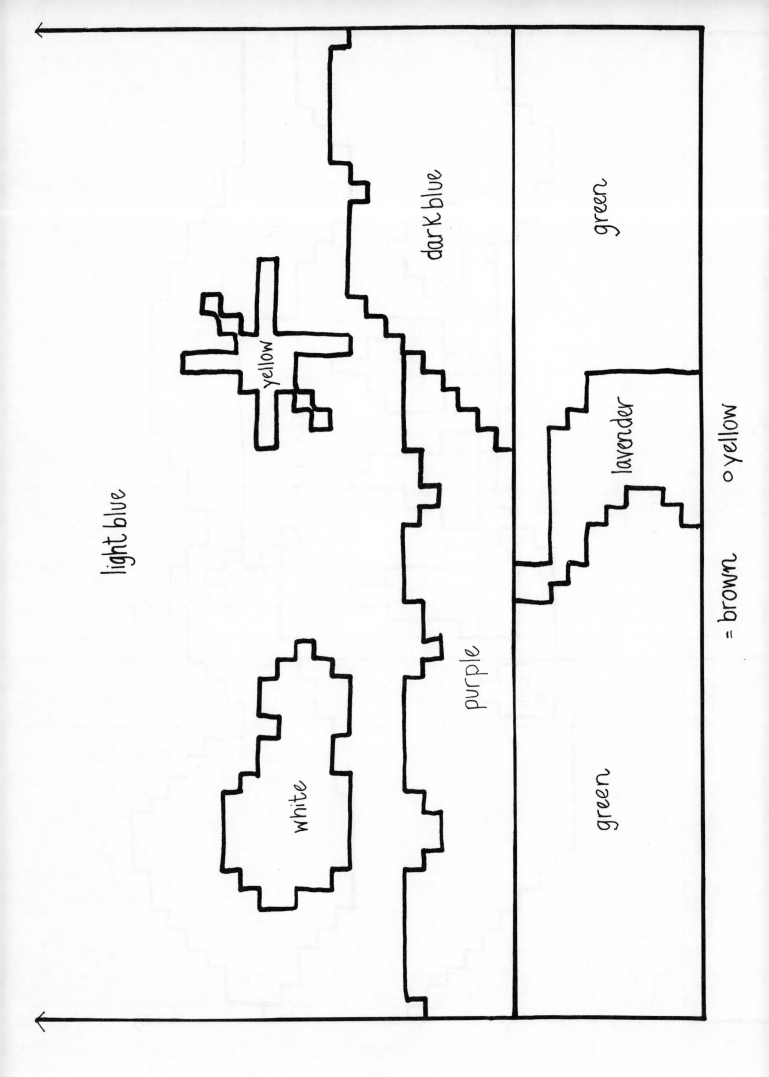

light blue

dark blue

green

yellow

lavender

purple

white

green

= brown   ○ yellow

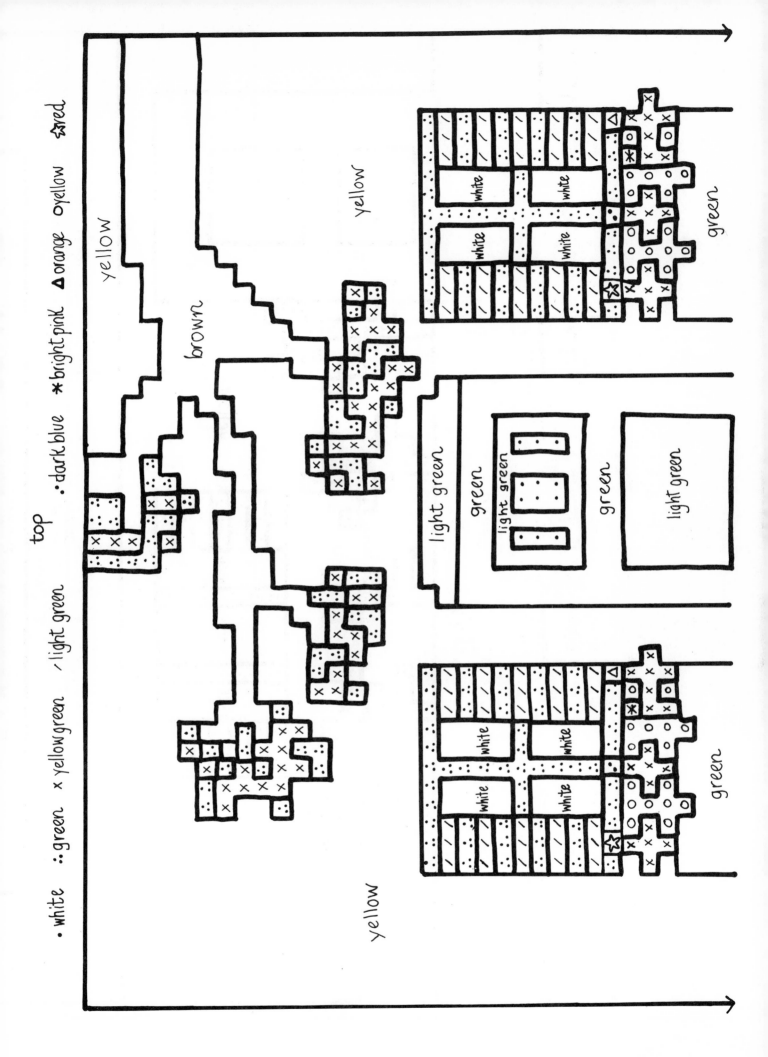

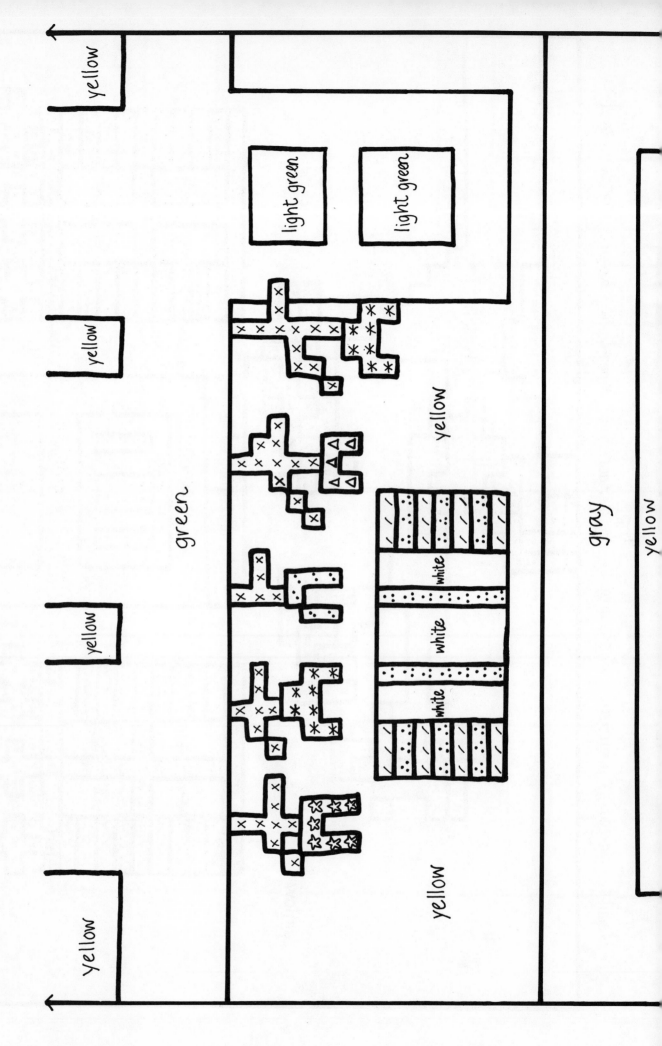

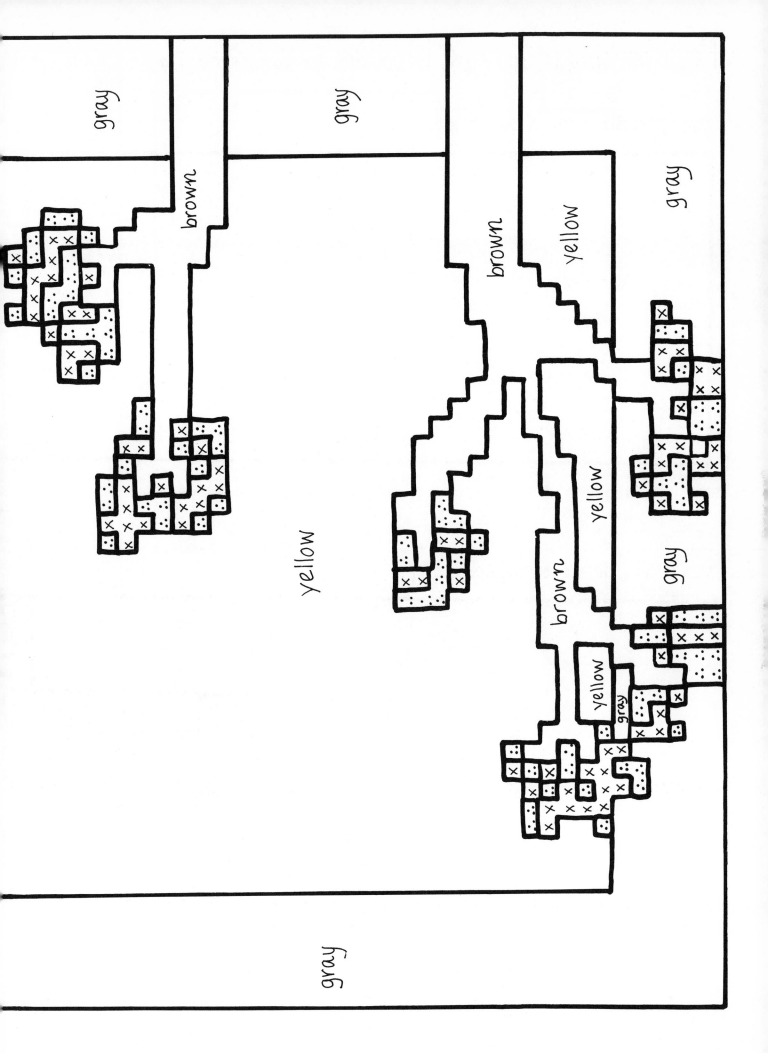

House handbag's strap - use this outline for all handbag straps

step 1. Trace this section of the outline first.

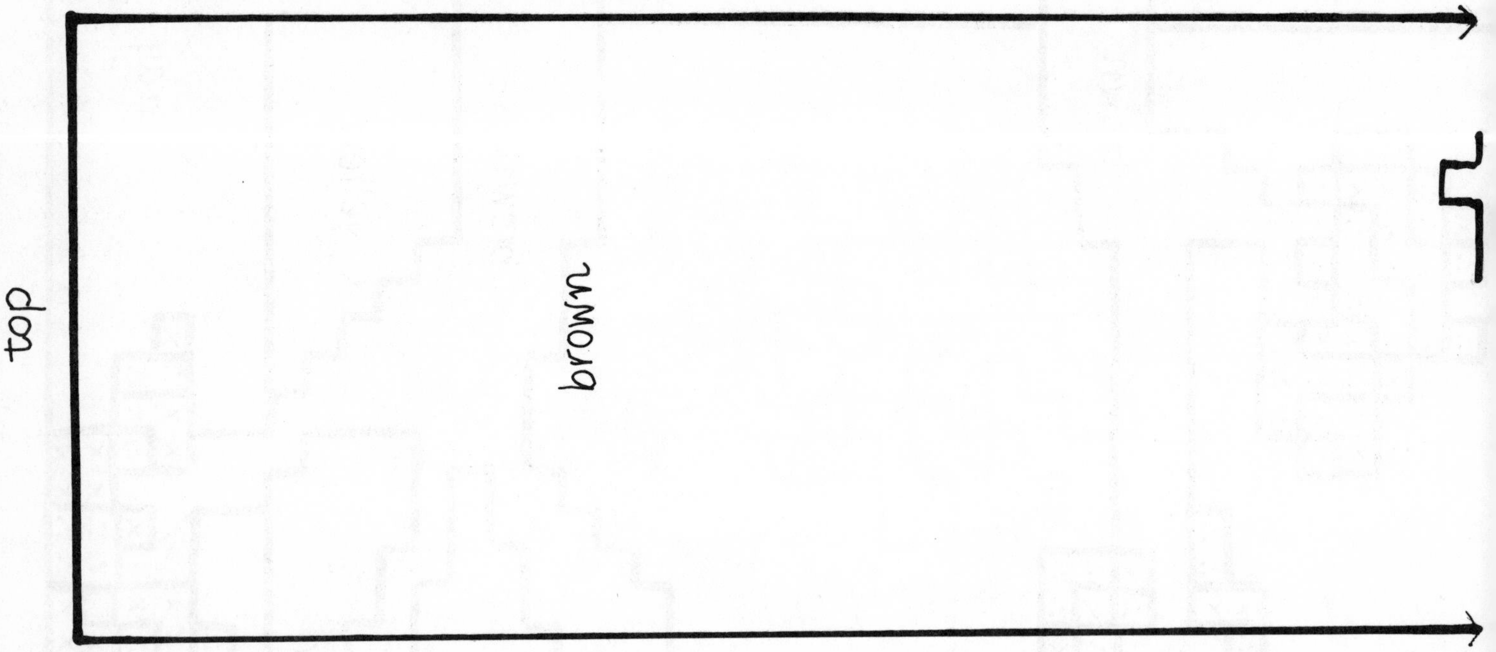

top

brown

step 3. Trace this section of the outline.

light blue

beige | yellow | yellow | yellow | beige | yellow | yellow | beige | yellow

yellow | yellow | yellow

yellow

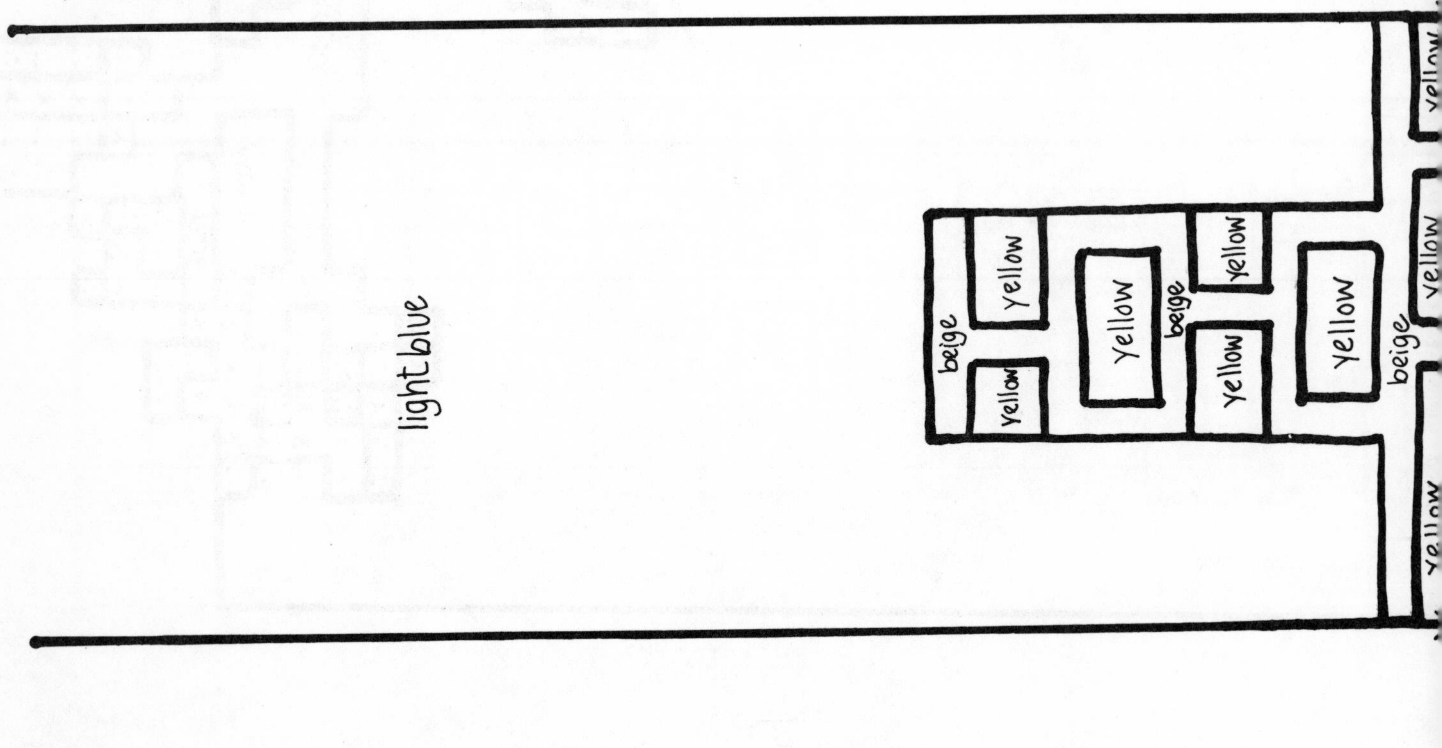

p 2. Trace this section of the outline adding 5 inches of outline in the gap.

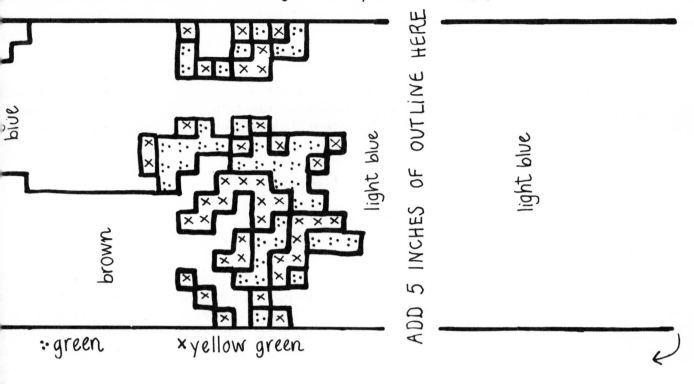

blue

light blue

ADD 5 INCHES OF OUTLINE HERE

light blue

brown

∴ green   × yellow green

Step 4. Trace this section of the outline last.

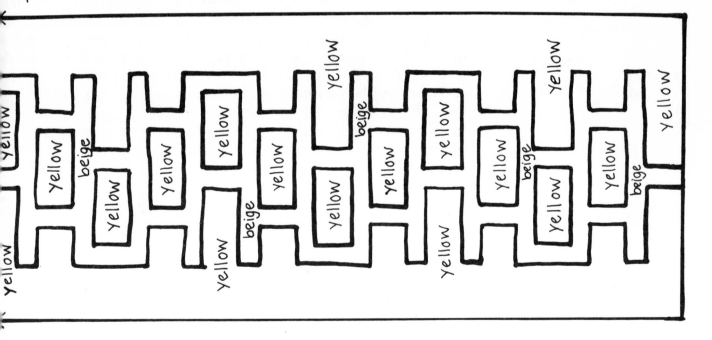

Navajo Carry-All Bag

Quickpoint is perfect for creating a unique, sturdy carry-all bag.
geometric design is easy to stitch since it has a repeating patter
triangles. The rich colors make the Navajo design handsome as w
practical.

You will need: Two pieces of No. 5 quickpoint canvas, each 16 inches by 16 inc
No. 14 tapestry needle for rug yarn
Yarn in red, dark green, dark blue, brown, blue-green, beige, dark or
purple
1/2 yard fabric for lining
3 yards fold-over braid for strap
Straight pins
Sewing needle and thread

Directions: **1.** Locate the center of the canvas by folding it in half and then in qua
Place the center of the canvas over the black star on the center edge o
right-hand page of the Navajo design. Make sure the center of the can
always over the black star as you trace the design. Working from the l
star across the page, start tracing the lines of the design (page 12) ont
canvas, counting the crossings on the canvas to be sure you are tracin
design correctly. Each symbol on the design represents a crossing. V
you have finished tracing the right-hand page, place the canvas on the
hand page so that the lines on the canvas meet the lines of the design o
left-hand page. To insure that your tracing will be correct, continu
lines forming the center diamond first. The diamond has two crossin
the top, two crossings at the side points, and is ten crossings wide. (
tinue to trace, working across the page. Paint in the colors of the d
(page 13) using the symbol color key. Add two complete rows of tria
at the top and bottom so that your finished carry-all bag will be abo
inches by 14 inches. Do the same on the second canvas.
2. Fold under and baste the margin of each of the canvases separately (
14). Do not sew the two pieces of your bag together at this time.
3. Quickpoint each canvas, then block.

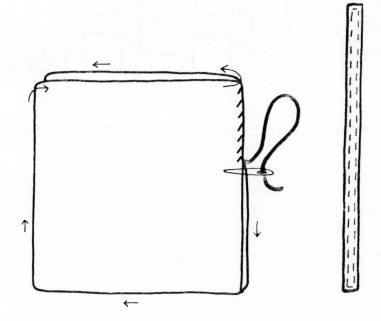

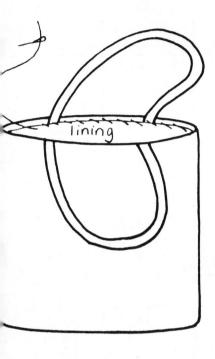

4. With right sides out, hold the two canvases together. Join the two edge lines with the binding stitch (pages 22-23) worked in dark blue yarn. Start at the top corner and stitch the two edge lines together, working towards the bottom. Bind across the bottom, then up the other side. Bind around the top edge of the opening of your bag.

5. To make the straps, iron the fold-over braid out flat; it will be about an inch wide. Cut the braid into four equal pieces, each one two feet long. Machine sew two pieces of braid together along the edges of both sides and both ends. This creates a sturdy strap. Sew the other two pieces of braid together in the same way.

6. Measure three inches in from a side seam of your bag. With two inches of strap inside the bag, pin the strap to the top edge of the bag. Pin the other end of the strap three inches in from the other side seam. Turn the bag over and pin the second strap in the same way. Shorten the straps if you prefer. With sewing needle and double thread, sew the straps in place by stitching through the quickpoint.

7. Fold the lining fabric in half with right sides together and trim the width to the width of the bag. Baste up the sides, sewing half an inch from the edge of the fabric. Put the lining into your carry-all bag. See how it fits. Take the lining out of the bag and machine sew the sides, adjusting the width of the seam as necessary.

8. Put the lining in your bag tucking in the top edge of the lining so that the raw edge does not show. With sewing needle and thread, use the hemming stitch to sew the lining to the top edge of the carry-all bag.

★ You can make a pocket in the lining of your carry-all bag by stitching a square of fabric to the outside of the lining. This is a great place to carry pens or a tiny notebook.

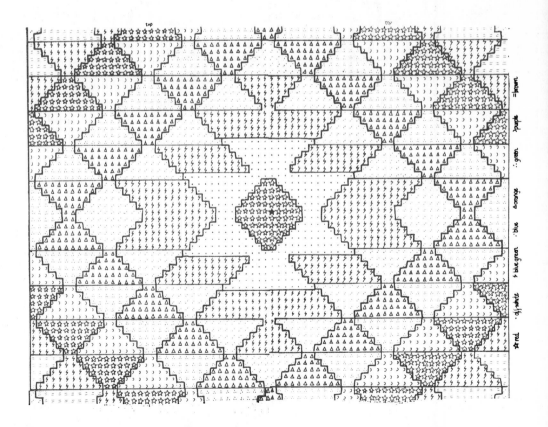

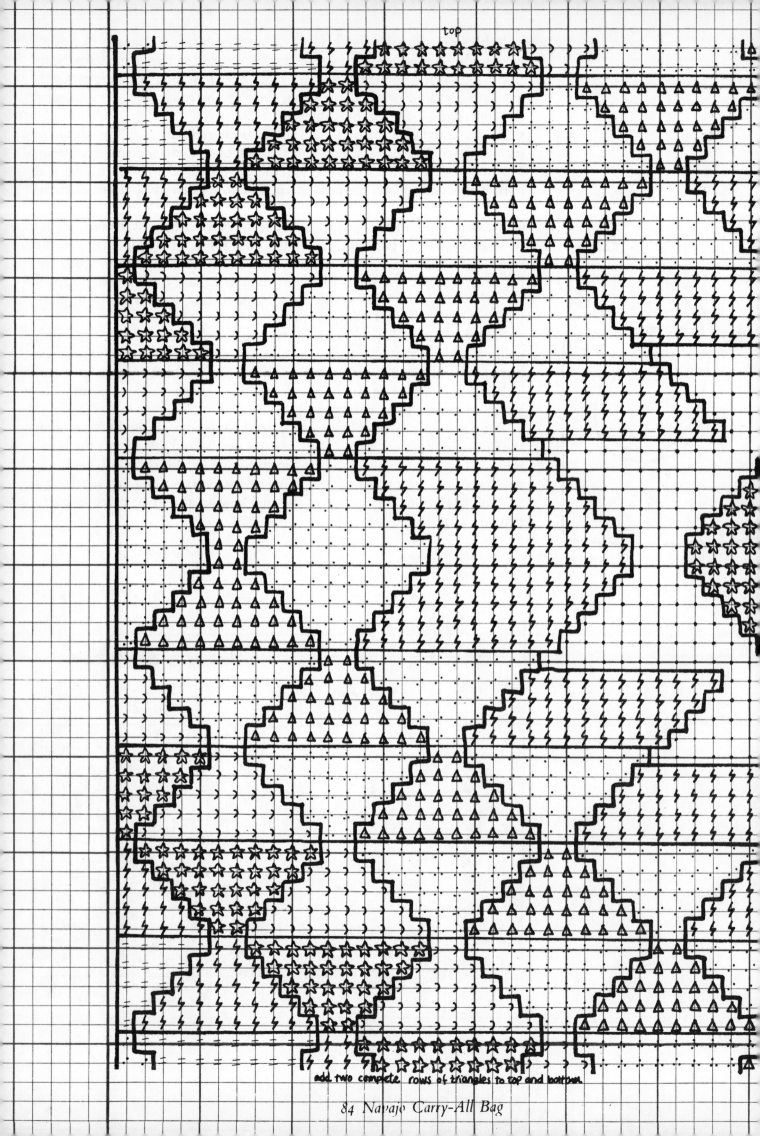

top

add two complete rows of triangles to top and bottom

84 Navajo Carry-All Bag

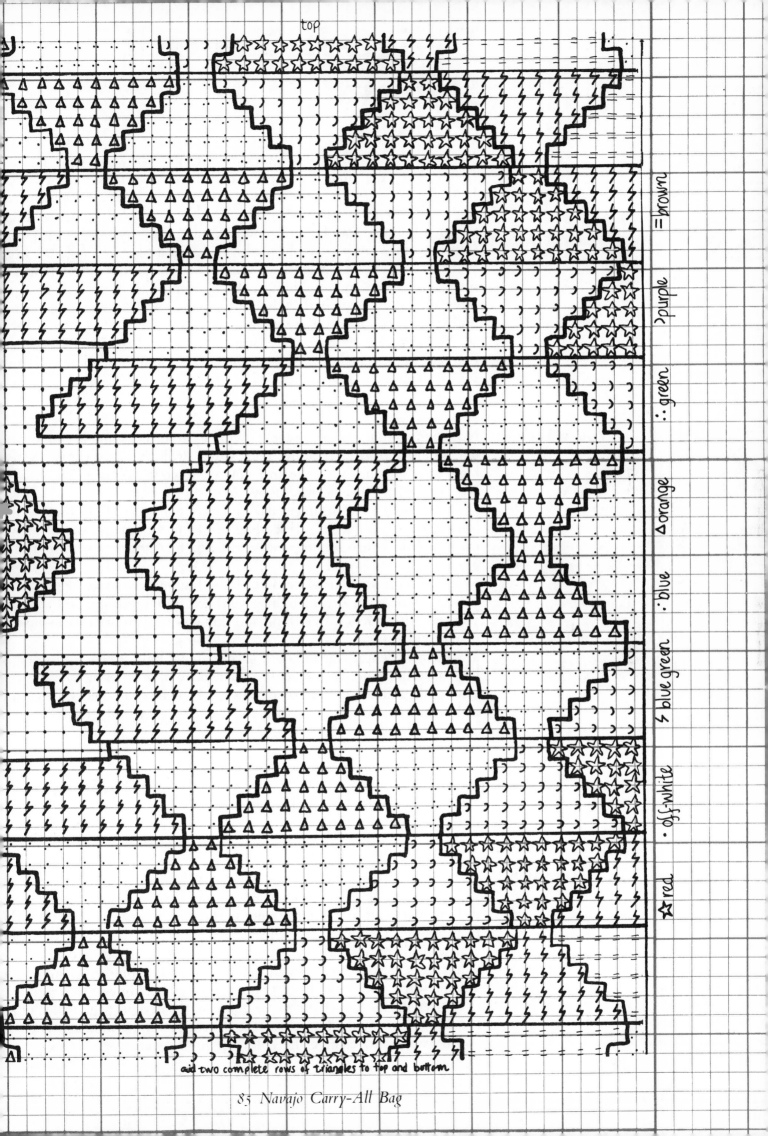

top

=brown

>purple

:: green

△orange

·: blue

⚡ blue green

· off-white

☆ red

and two complete rows of triangles to top and bottom

85 Navajo Carry-All Bag

Design-It-Yourself Pillows

You can design your own quickpoint canvas showing your family friends doing the things they love in their favorite surroundings. A Desi It-Yourself pillow is your chance to create a charming primitive quickpoint. You design it yourself! We have included three backgrou designs: hillside, seaside, and mountainside, and filled them with sam figures to inspire you. We have also included a page of suggested obj that you can add or replace as you like. Design a family pillow that is u quely your own by combining a background and figures. A Design Yourself pillow is a perfect housewarming gift and since it is done quickpoint, you'll finish it on time!

★ You can also design a truly original carry-all bag. Paint your pict onto canvases 22 inches wide by 16 inches long and proceed to step 2 in Navajo Carry-all Bag project.

You will need: No. 5 quickpoint canvas, 22 inches wide by 16 inches long. If you are m: ing a pillow from "Creating Your Own Projects," buy canvas 2 inc bigger on all sides than the size you want your pillow to be.
No. 14 tapestry needle for rug yarn
Hillside design: yarn in green, dark green, light green, light blue, yello brown, gray, red, white, dark blue, bright pink, orange; strands of yc favorite colors for clothing and skin color for figures; yarn-for-detail gray.
Seaside design: yarn in white, light blue, blue-green, aqua, beige, brov yellow, dark blue, green, light green, red, pink, orange, and strands your favorite colors for clothing and skin color for figures; yarn-for-det in red and brown.
Mountainside design: yarn in dark green, green, light green, light blue, s blue, medium blue, dark blue, lavender, brown, orange, light orange, y low, pink, red, white strands of yarn in your favorite colors for clothi and skin color for figures; yarn-for-detail in gray and green.
Yarn-for-detail in colors needed for adding other objects, and No. tapestry needle
Sewing needle and thread
2 yards of trim (optional)
1/2 yard fabric for the back of the pillow
A bag of pillow stuffing

Directions: 1. Trace the background design you have chosen onto your canvas (pa 12). Trace the figures and other objects you have selected onto the canv if those you want to include are not in the design you are using, trace th from another Design-It-Yourself page. Have fun placing the figures whe you want them; just don't put them too close to the bottom of the desig Adult faces are two stitches wide and three stitches long. All arms and le are one stitch wide. The height of a figure can be adjusted by lengtheni or shortening the legs. Paint in the colors of the design (page 13). Use yo favorite colors for the figures' clothes; paint the house to match your ov and if you want, change the colors of the flowers.

2. Fold masking tape over the edges of the canvas (page 10).

3. Quickpoint the canvas. You can use the Stitches for Fun to add texture to areas of solid color such as the hillsides and mountains.

4. Block the quickpointed canvas.

5. Stitches for detail: to make a figure's hair use quickpoint yarn and three or four straight stitches; experiment with varied stitch lengths to create different hairstyles. Use two threads of Persian yarn or any other type of thin yarn and stitches for detail to complete the design where necessary: the outline of the tennis racquet, the kite string, the fishing line, and tufts of grass. Add other details if you want to: put the dog on a leash, apples on the trees, or rays on the sun.

6. The instructions which follow can also be used to make a pillow as small as a sachet or as large as a floor pillow. Machine stay stitch through the margin of unworked canvas 1/4-inch from the worked quickpoint. This will keep the canvas from raveling.

7. Cut the fabric for the back of the pillow so that it is the same size as your canvas.

8. If you want to put trim around a pillow: with right side of the quickpointed canvas up, baste the trim to the quickpoint stitch nearest the margin of canvas as shown in the illustration.

9. Place right sides of the backing fabric and quickpointed canvas together and machine sew through the row of quickpoint stitches nearest the margin of canvas and the fabric. Sew around three sides of the pillow, turning the corners of the fourth side, but leaving an opening for stuffing.

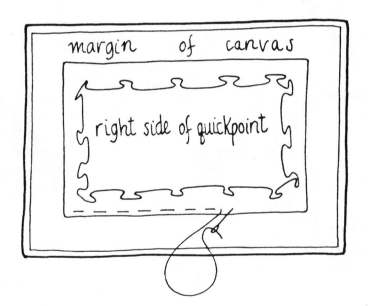

10. Trim the margin of canvas and fabric to within 1 1/4 inch of the worked quickpoint. Trim the seamed corners diagonally and turn the pillow inside out. Stuff the pillow and with sewing needle and thread, use the hemming stitch to sew the pillow closed.

★ If you have chosen the mountainside for your design, add pine needles to the pillow stuffing; it will be a fragrant reminder of your favorite mountain retreat.

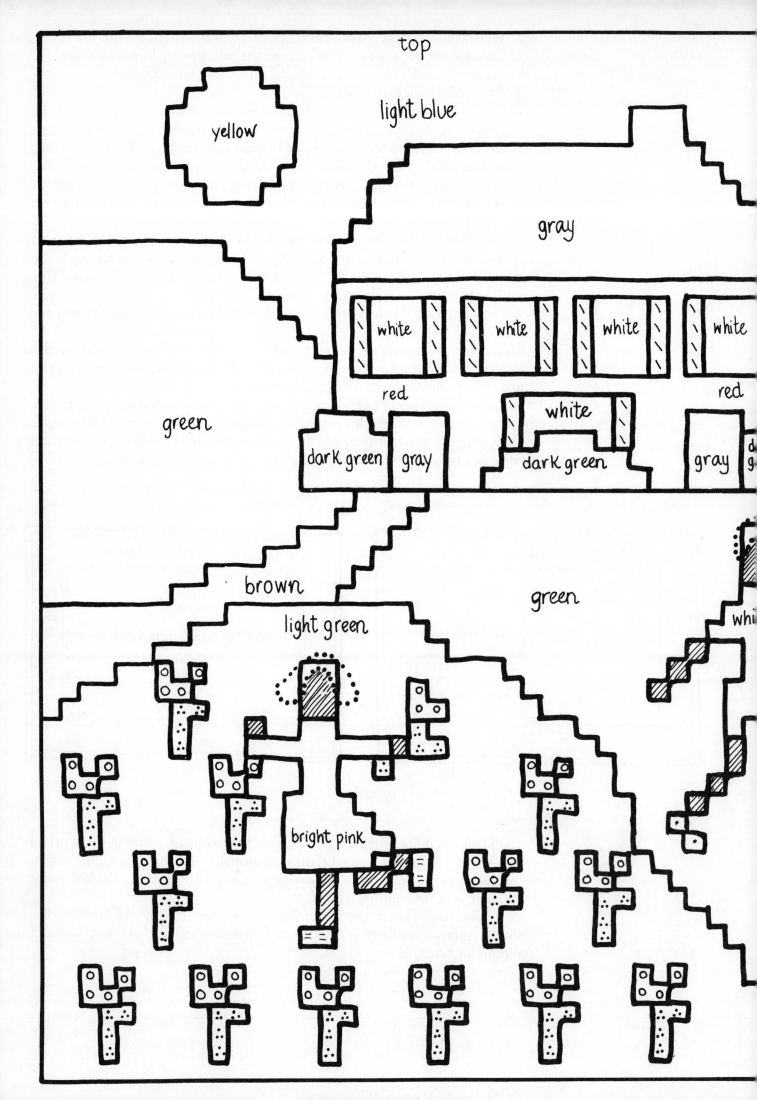

top

yellow

light blue

gray

green

white white white white

red red

dark green gray white dark green gray

brown

green

light green whi

bright pink

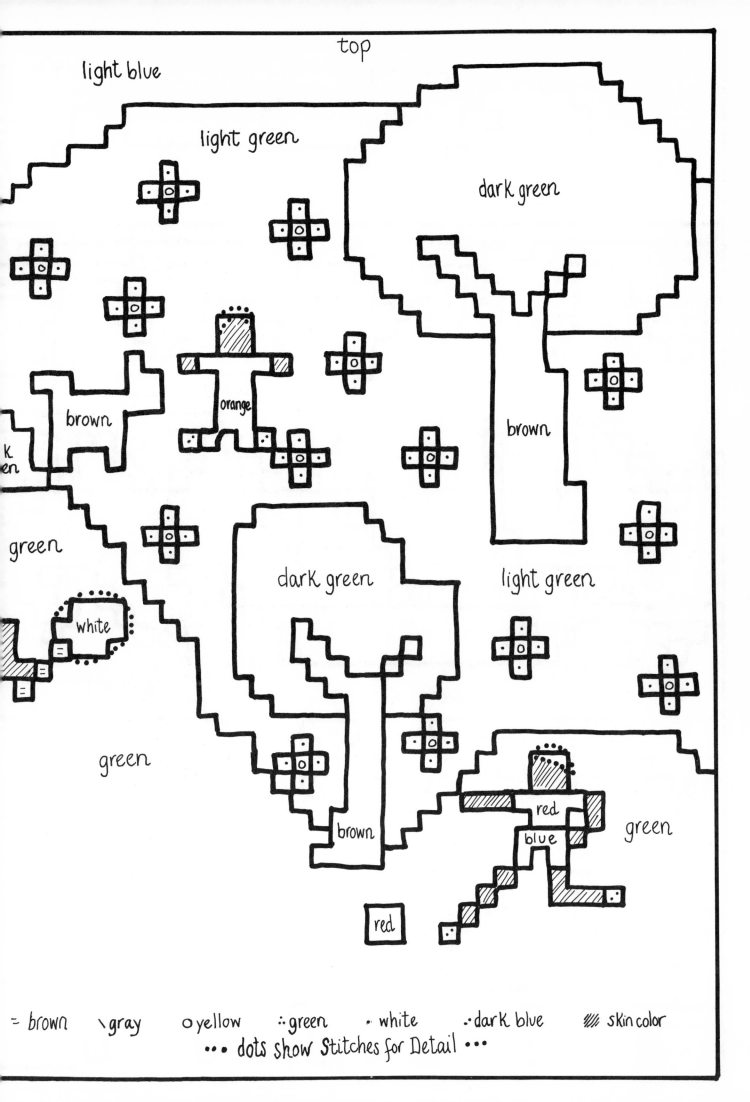

top

light blue

light green

dark green

brown

orange

green

brown

light green

white

dark green

green

green

brown

red

blue

red

green

= brown   \ gray   o yellow   ∴ green   • white   • dark blue   ⫻ skin color
••• dots show Stitches for Detail •••

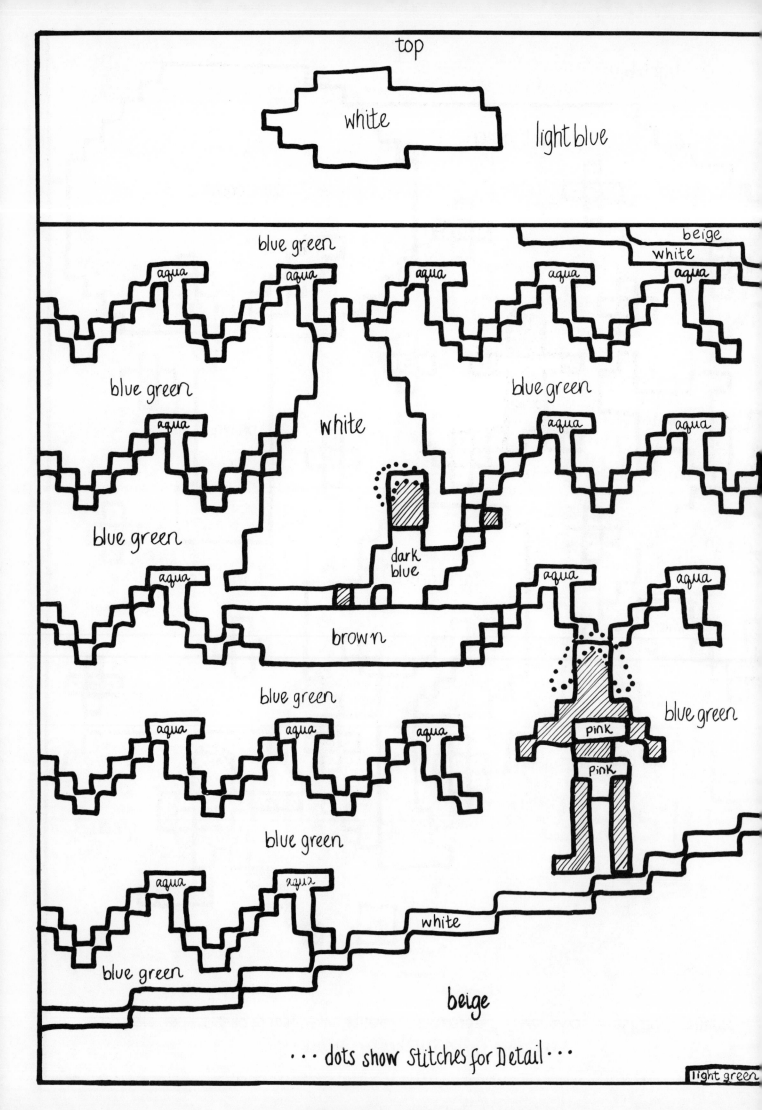

top

white

light blue

blue green

beige
white

aqua aqua aqua aqua aqua

blue green blue green

white aqua aqua

blue green

dark
blue

aqua aqua aqua

brown

blue green blue green

aqua aqua aqua pink

pink

blue green

blue green

aqua aqua

white

blue green

beige

··· dots show stitches for Detail ···

light green

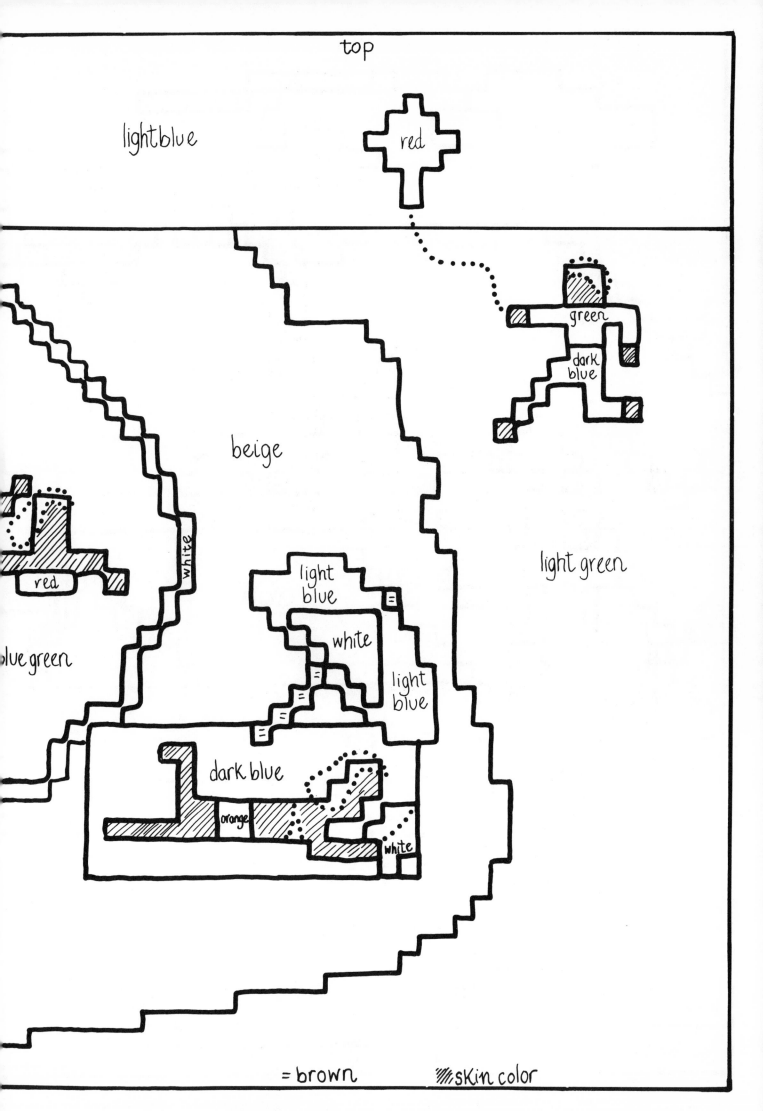

top

lightblue

red

green

dark blue

beige

light green

red

white

blue green

light blue

white

light blue

dark blue

orange

white

= brown

skin color

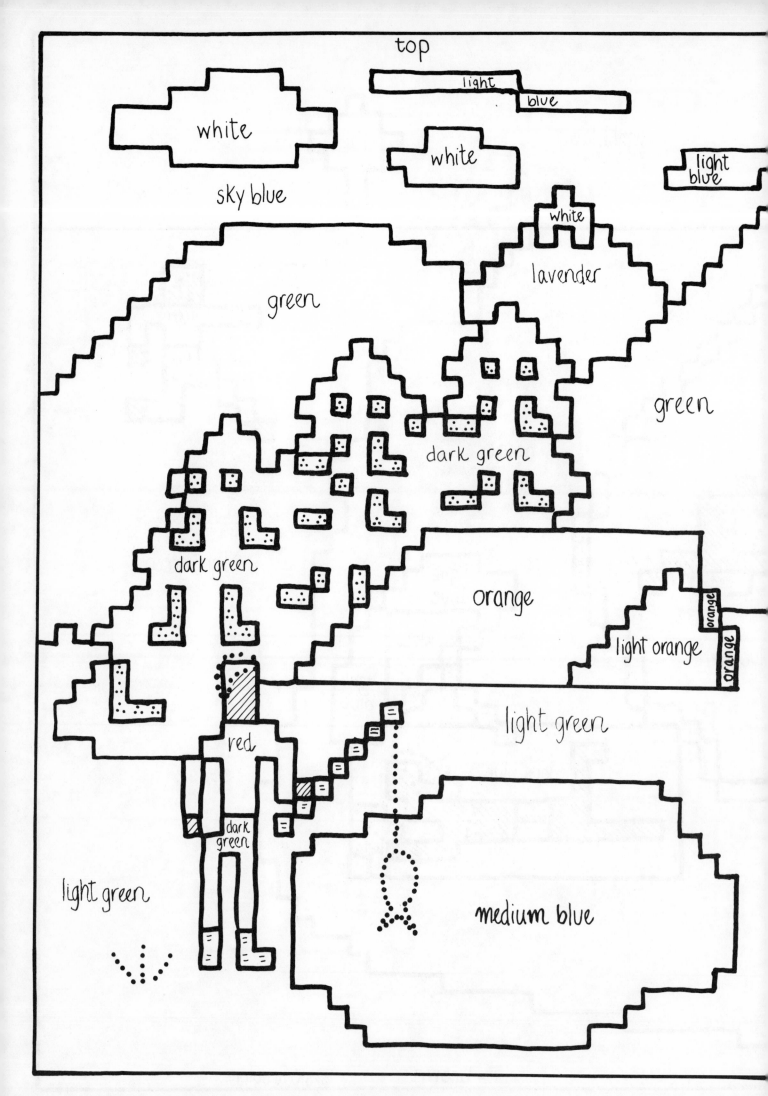

top

white

light blue

white

light blue

sky blue

green

white

lavender

green

dark green

dark green

orange

light orange

orange

orange

light green

red

dark green

light green

medium blue

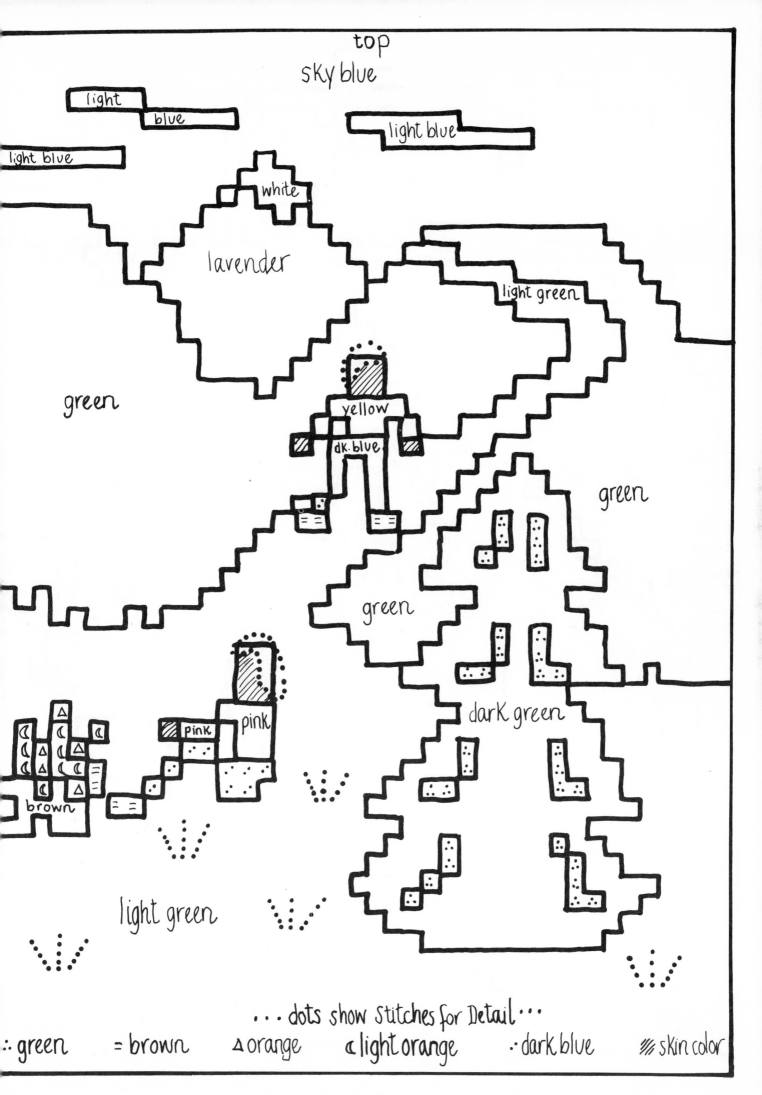

top

sky blue

light
blue

light blue

light blue

white

lavender

light green

green

yellow

dk. blue

green

green

dark green

pink

pink

brown

light green

··· dots show stitches for Detail ···

∴ green   = brown   △ orange   ⊄ light orange   · dark blue   ⫽ skin color

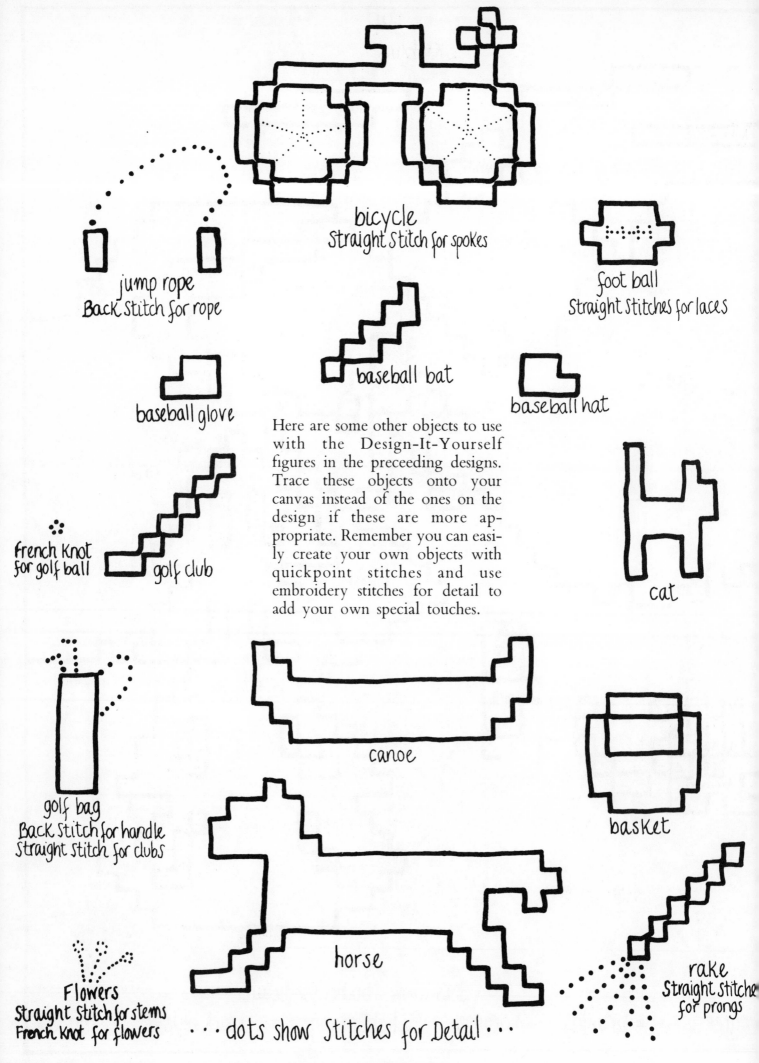

bicycle
Straight Stitch for spokes

jump rope
Back Stitch for rope

foot ball
Straight Stitches for laces

baseball bat

baseball glove

baseball hat

Here are some other objects to use with the Design-It-Yourself figures in the preceeding designs. Trace these objects onto your canvas instead of the ones on the design if these are more appropriate. Remember you can easily create your own objects with quickpoint stitches and use embroidery stitches for detail to add your own special touches.

cat

French Knot
for golf ball

golf club

golf bag
Back Stitch for handle
Straight stitch for clubs

canoe

basket

horse

Flowers
Straight stitch for stems
French Knot for flowers

··· dots show Stitches for Detail ···

rake
Straight stitches
for prongs

How To Make A Quickpoint Kit

A quickpoint kit has everything: a painted canvas, needle, and yarn. It is a great gift for people who love to stitch because they can start to work right away. A group of quickpoint kits also provides a welcome addition to any bazaar.

You will need:
Masking tape or fabric bias binding
Painted quickpoint canvas
No. 14 tapestry needle for rug yarn
Clear plastic bag large enough to hold the painted canvas
Yarn in the colors of the design
Ribbon or rickrack
Heavy white paper or poster board (optional)

Directions for assembling:

1. Fold masking tape around the edges of the painted canvas or, as an extra custom touch, baste a bright-colored bias binding over the edges of the canvas. (The tape or binding can be removed for projects requiring folded edges).

2. Put the needle through the canvas.

3. Place the canvas in the plastic bag so that the painted design is shown to best advantage. Your painted design will be highlighted even more if you back the canvas with a piece of white paper or white poster board.

4. Twist the yarn into attractive bunches and arrange them in the bag.

5. Tie the top of the plastic bag with yarn, ribbon, or rickrack. Or make a top for your quickpoint kit by folding heavy white paper the width of the plastic bag and stapling through the folded top with the plastic bag sandwiched in between. Across the top, write: "Quickpoint Kit by Susan" or "Happy Birthday, Hannah."

Creating Your Own Projects

Now that you have enjoyed making the quickpoint projects in this book you are ready to use your imagination to create your own quickpoint projects. There are unlimited possibilities for creating original quickpointed items. Most of the designs on the preceeding pages can be used for other projects as well. Study the chart below to see new ways to use the designs. The chart shows which designs and projects combine effectively.

Follow these step-by-step instructions to combine designs and projects:

1. Decide which of the *designs* you want to stitch. With the chart as your guide, select the suitable *project* you want to make.
2. Turn to the page listed with the *project* you want to make and buy canvas in the size indicated. Trace the *project's* outline onto the canvas as described on page 12, step 4.
3. *Turn to the design* you have chosen and place the canvas over the design in the book. Place the canvas so that the *design* will attractively fill the space within the outline. Trace the lines of the *design* onto your canvas and paint in the colors of the *design* as described on pages 12, step 5.
4. Turn to the *project* and proceed according to the directions for the *project* starting at step No. 2.

Creating your own projects

★ shows the designs and projects which are presented together in the book.

☆ shows suggested combinations of designs and projects.

* shows designs and projects which can be combined with some initiative.

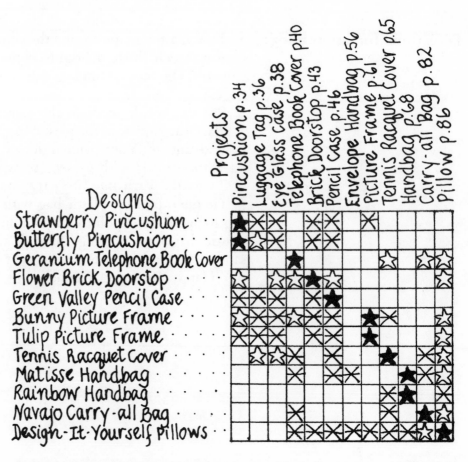

Designs / Projects	Pincushion p.34	Luggage Tag p.36	Eye Glass Case p.38	Telephone Book Cover p.40	Brick Doorstop p.43	Pencil Case p.46	Envelope Handbag p.56	Picture Frame p.61	Tennis Racquet Cover p.65	Handbag p.68	Carry-all Bag p.82	Pillow p.86
Strawberry Pincushion	★	×	×	×		×	×		×			
Butterfly Pincushion	★	☆	×	×		×			×			
Geranium Telephone Book Cover			×	★		×		☆			☆	☆
Flower Brick Doorstop		☆	×	☆	★	☆						☆
Green Valley Pencil Case			×	×	×	★						
Bunny Picture Frame		×	×					★		☆		☆
Tulip Picture Frame		☆	×					★				☆
Tennis Racquet Cover		☆	×					☆	★			
Matisse Handbag			×						×	★	×	
Rainbow Handbag			×							★	×	
Navajo Carry-all Bag			×						×	×	★	
Design-It-Yourself Pillows				×		×	×		×		☆	★

Four Versatile Designs

By the time you have created a few of your own quickpoint projects, you are bound to be an enthusiastic quickpointer. So, especially for you, we have created Four Versatile Designs to challenge your creativity.

You can use these designs to make almost any project in this book. Look at the Four Versatile Designs and color photographs to see how delightful these designs are. You can trace the outline from any previous project design and fill it in this time with any of the Four Versatile Designs in your favorite colors. Try making a glasses case, tennis racquet cover, pillow, or anything else on the chart. Study the chart below to see the possible combinations and decide on an original project uniquely your own. Follow the step-by-step instructions on the preceding page to combine designs and projects. You can trace, paint, and quickpoint these designs to make your own quickpoint creations.

Each design has symbols to tell you what color each crossing should be. Each symbol on the design represents a crossing. Remember to count the crossings on your canvas to insure that you are tracing correctly.

The Patchwork design is made up of squares which you can rearrange to make many different designs. The Ribbons, Woven Basket, and Indian designs are striking geometrics that look marvelous when stitched in the suggested colors or in colors of your own choosing. Any of these designs can be extended to fill in any size outline. To do this, trace the design onto your canvas, then move the canvas so that the lines that have been traced onto your canvas meet the lines of the design in the book, and continue to trace.

Now you know all there is to know about quickpointing. The rest is up to you. And the sky is the limit!

Creating your own projects from the four Versatile Designs

☆ shows designs and projects which can be combined. Use your judgment to place the canvas so that the design attractively fills the space within the outline. You may have to repeat the design to fill in the outline or you may trace only part of the design to fill in the outline.

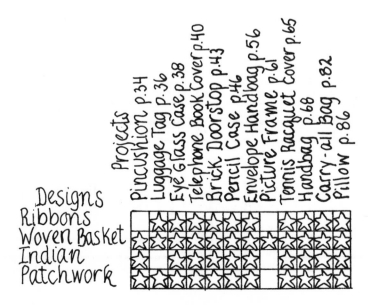

97

top

98 Ribbons Design

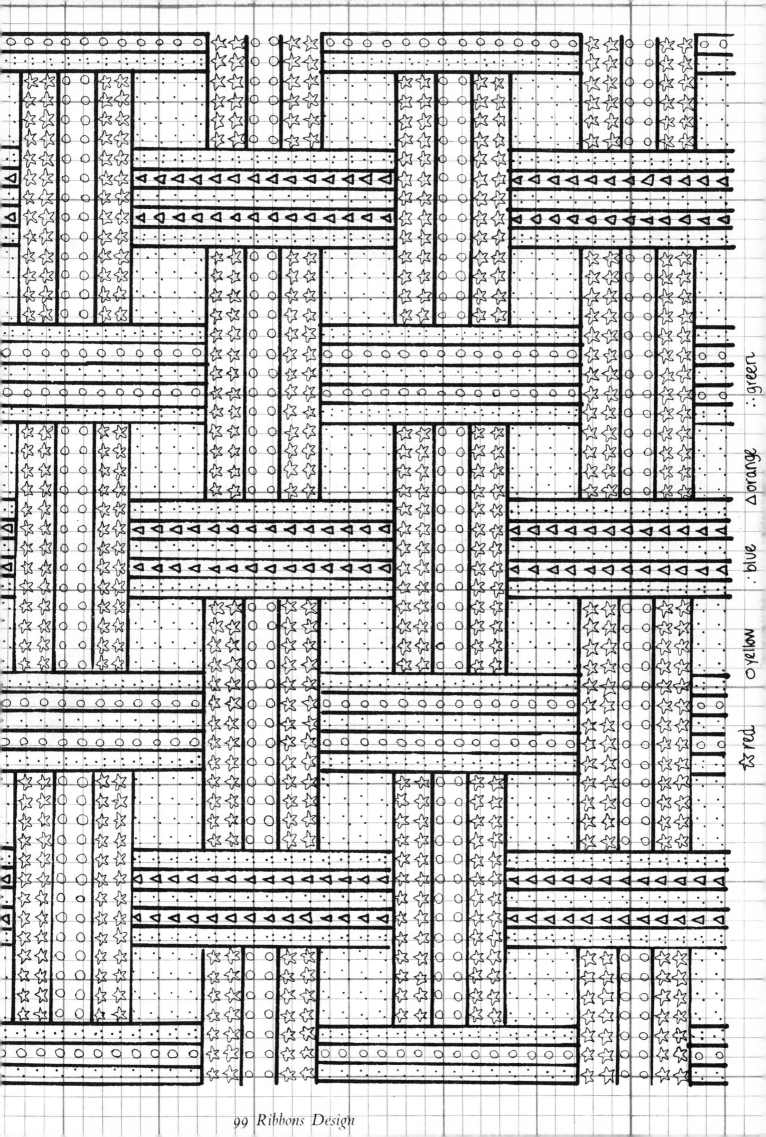

☆ red   ○ yellow   . blue   △ orange   :: green

99 Ribbons Design

top

ˇbeige   =brown   ·white

100 Woven Basket Design

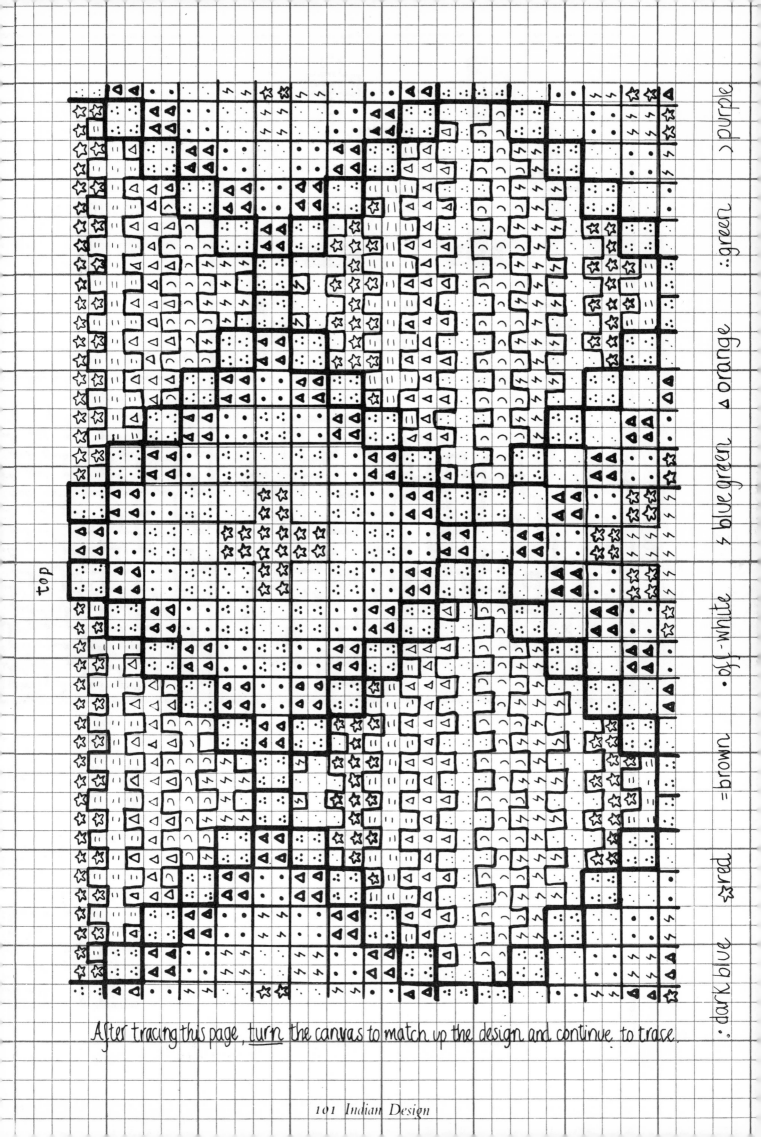

top

After tracing this page, <u>turn</u> the canvas to match up the design and continue to trace.

> purple
:: green
△ orange
↕ blue green
· off-white
= brown
☆ red
·: dark blue

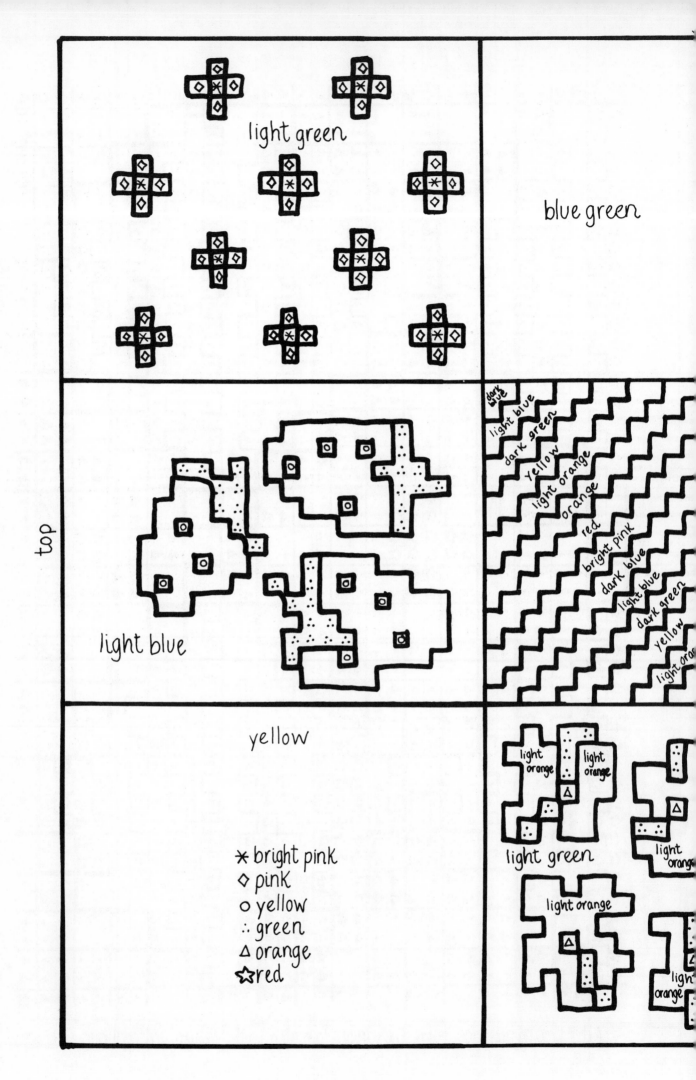

light green

blue green

top

light blue

yellow

dark blue
light blue
dark green
yellow
light orange
orange
red
bright pink
dark blue
light blue
dark green
yellow
light orange

light orange
light orange
light green
light orange
light orange
light orange

* bright pink
◇ pink
○ yellow
∴ green
△ orange
☆ red

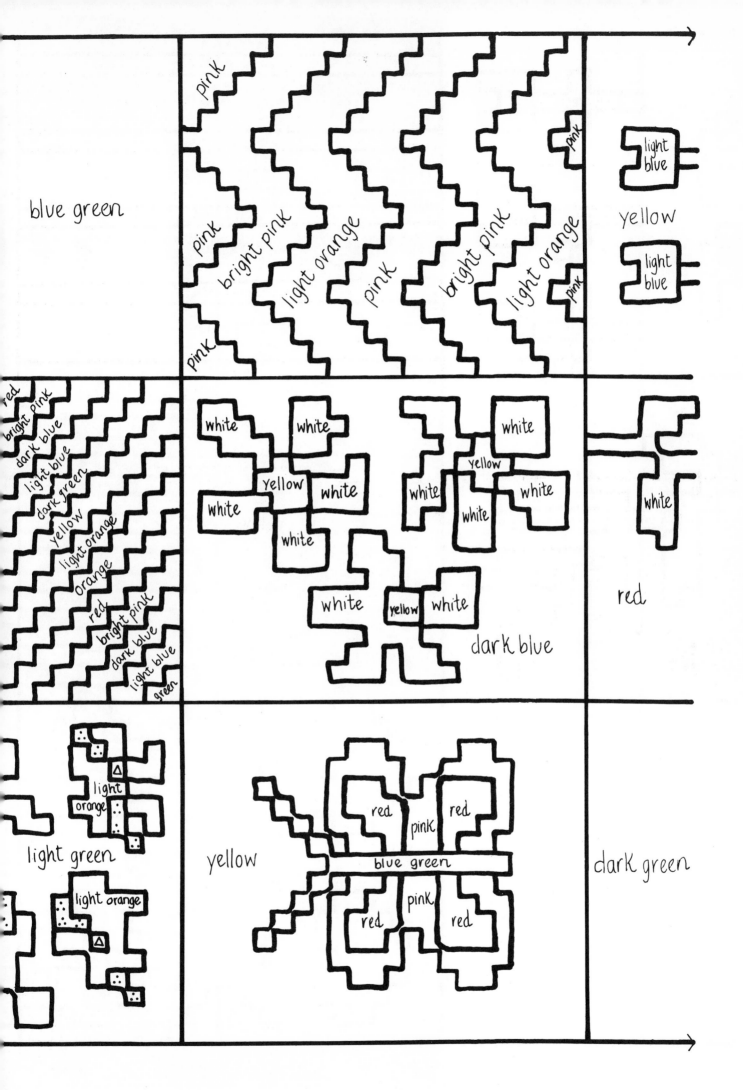

blue green

pink

pink

bright pink

light orange

pink

bright pink

light orange

pink

pink

light
blue

yellow

light
blue

red
bright pink
dark blue
light blue
dark green
yellow
light orange
orange
red
bright pink
dark blue
light blue
green

white

white

Yellow

white

White

white

white

white

yellow

white

white

white

white

yellow

white

dark blue

white

red

light
orange

light green

light orange

yellow

red

pink

red

blue green

red

pink

red

dark green

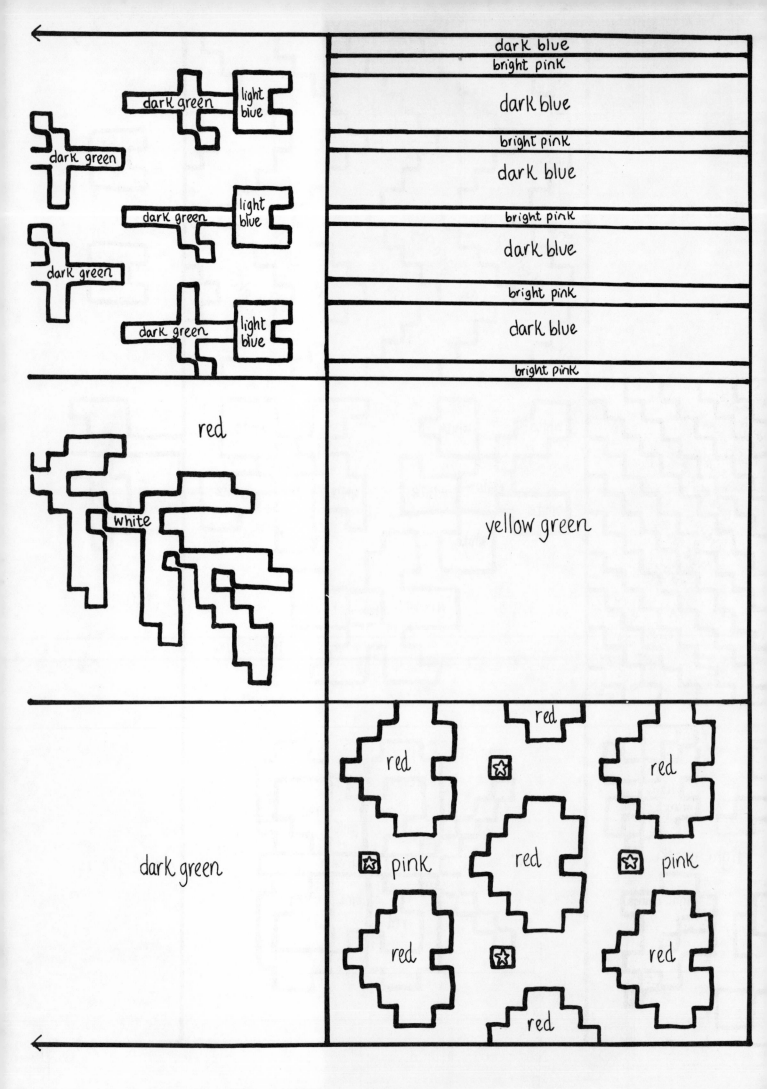